PATTERNS AND ELLIPSES

BY

LARRY JACOBS

TABLE OF CONTENTS

Table of Contents

PATTERNS AND ELLIPSES	1
PREFACE	8
IDEALISTIC PERCEPTIONS	9
WHAT IS IMPLIED BY TIME?	11
THE RULES OF TIME	13
MOVEMENT IN THE UNIVERSE	14
HOW THE MARKET PLACE WORKS	18
TYPES OF PEOPLE WHO BUY AND SELL STOCK	19
PERSONAL FEELINGS	21
OVERTRADING	22
HOW DO YOU KNOW WHAT THE MARKET WILL DO TOMORROW?	23
LAWS OF THE MARKET	25
METHODS OF BUYING	26
KNOW YOUR STOCKS	28
KNOW THE TYPES OF CHARTS TO USE	29
BAR CHART TIME SEPARATION	30
BAR CHART – STENGTH	31
BAR CHART - SWING	32
CANDLESTICK CHARTS	33
GANN SWING BAR CHART	34
SWING CHART IMPOSED ON REGULAR BAR CHART	36
GANN SWING CHART	40
BARROS SWINGS	41
LINE CHARTS	42

RANGE CHARTS	43
POINT AND FIGURE CHARTS	45
KAGI SWING CHART	47
CALENDAR DAYS VS TRADING DAYS	49
GANN FAN ON CALENDAR BASED CHARTS	51
GANN FAN ON TRADING DAY BASED CHARTS	53
GANN FAN ON CALENDAR BASED CHARTS WITH REACTIONS	54
GANN FAN ON TRADING DAY BASED CHARTS WITH REACTIONS	55
USING THE GANN FAN WITH ASTROLOGY	56
ZERO POINT – WEEKLY CHARTS ON DEC OATS	57
SQUARING RANGE – MONTHLY CHART ON DEC COCOA	58
GANN FAN GEOMETRIC ANGLES	59
GANN SQUARES	61
GANN SQUARES EXTENDED	63
THE BIBLICAL CIRCLE	64
35-DAY CALENDAR TIME CYCLE – DUPONT	66
SAME TIME COUNTS	67
50-WEEKLY CYCLE	68
37.5 WEEKLY CYCLE	69
25 WEEKLY CYCLE	70
17 WEEKLY CYCLE	71
12.5 WEEKLY CYCLE	72
8.5 WEEKLY CYCLE	73
6.25 WEEKLY CYCLE	74
CONVERT WEEKLY CYCLE INTO 21.87 DAYS	75
CONVERT WEEKLY CYCLE INTO 14.58 DAYS	76

CONVERT WEEKLY CYCLE INTO 10.93 DAYS	77
CONVERT WEEKLY CYCLE INTO 7.29 DAYS	78
CONVERT WEEKLY CYCLE INTO 3.65 DAYS	79
ASPECTS	80
ASPECTS TIED TO CYCLES	82
SUN SEXTILE MARS	84
SUN SEXTILE JUPITER	85
SUN SEXTILE SATURN	86
SUN SEXTILE URANUS	87
SUN SEXTILE NEPTUNE	88
SUN SEXTILE PLUTO	89
VENUS SEXTILE MARS	90
VENUS SEXTILE JUPITER	91
VENUS SEXTILE SATURN	92
VENUS SEXTILE URANUS	93
VENUS SEXTILE NEPTUNE	94
VENUS SEXTILE JUPITER	95
ASTROLOGICAL TIMING	96
VISUAL EPHEMERIS	98
ASTROLOGICAL CRITICAL DEGREES	101
GANN PLANETARY LINES	103
SQUARE OF NINE	105
STATIC SQUARE OF NINE	106
PYRAPOINT	108
CONCENTRIC CIRCLES - TIME	114
CONCENTRIC CIRCLES – PRICE	116
FIBONACCI ARCS	117
FIBONACCI FAN	118

PRICE EXTENSIONS	119
PRICE RETRACEMENTS	120
TIME EXTENSIONS	121
TIME RETRACEMENTS	123
ANDREW'S PITCHFORK	124
ADX INDICATOR	125
BOLLINGER BANDS	127
COMMODITY CHANNEL INDEX	128
KELTNER CHANNELS	130
MACD INDICATOR	131
MOVING AVERAGE BANDS	132
MOVING AVERAGES and CYCLES	133
MOVING AVERAGE MOMENTUM	134
PARABOLIC STOP AND REVERSE	135
5/25 PRICE OSCILLATOR	137
RATE OF CHANGE	138
RELATIVE STRENGTH INDEX	139
STOCHASTICS	140
TEMPERATURE	141
WILLIAMS %R	143
LINEAR REGRESSION	145
HISTORICAL VOLATILITY RATIO	146
STANDARD DEVIATION	147
VOLUME ADVANCE DECLINE OSCILLATOR	148
MIDAS INDICATOR	149
MONEY FLOW INDEX	150
OPEN INTEREST	152
VOLUME	156

PRICE MOVES	157
GAPS	159
OTHER GAPS	161
ELLIPSES	162
DIFFERENT SIZES OF ELLIPSES	164
CHANNELS WITH ELLIPSES	165
CHANNELS WITH ELLIPSES – CHANGE OF TREND	166
SIDEWAYS TRENDING CHANNEL	167
CHANGE OF DIRECTION CHANNEL	168
FORMATIONS – EGG OF COLUMBUS	169
EXAMPLE OF DINNER WITH REAL-CHART	174
ELLIPSES WORK WITH STANDARD FORMATIONS	175
BROADENING BOTTOM FORMATION	176
BROADENING TOP FORMATION	177
RIGHT ANGLE FORMATION	178
RIGHT ANGLE FORMATION – 5 POINTS TOUCHING	179
RIGHT ANGLE DESCENDING FORMATION	180
BROADENING ASCENDING WEDGE FORMATION	181
THREE BUMP BOTTOM	182
THREE BUMP TOP	183
CUP AND HANDLE	184
GAP & BOUNCE	185
DIAMOND TOPS AND BOTTOMS	186
DOUBLE BOTTOMS	187
DOUBLE BOTTOM FAILURE	188
DOUBLE TOP	189
PENNANTS	190
FLAGS	191

HEAD AND SHOULDERS BOTTOMS 192
HEAD AND SHOULDERS TOP 193
INSIDE BAR 194
ISLAND REVERSALS 195
MEASURED OBJECTIVE DOWN 196
MEASURED OBJECTIVE UP 197
ONE-DAY REVERSAL 198
OUTSIDE BAR 199
TWO REVERSE BARS 200
TWO REVERSE BARS ON WEEKLY CHARTS 201
RECTANGLE BOTTOMS 202
RECTANGLE TOPS 203
ROUNDED BOTTOM 204
ROUNDED TOP 205
ROUNDING CORRECTION UPTREND 206
ROUNDED CORRECTION DOWNTREND 207
ASCENDING TRIANGLE 208
DESCENDING TRIANGLE 209
SYMMETRICAL BOTTOM TRIANGLES 210
SYMMETRICAL TOP TRIANGLES 211
TRIPLE BOTTOMS 212
TRIPLE TOP 213
FALLING WEDGE 214
RISING WEDGE 215
REVERSAL BAR 216
SUMMARY 217

PREFACE

This book concerns itself with a highly technical subject, the subject of technical analysis of the financial market. This book specifically deals with ellipses and pattern formations used for trading the markets. It also covers many other technical analysis tools that can be used effectively by the trader. This book is not intended for the casual reader, but for the student of the market that is willing to spend the necessary time for study, research and back testing of this methodology.

This book will reveal the mathematics underlying the subject matter and therefore I consider it a scientific book for that reason. This book teaches a methodology that gives you a clear way of detecting and identifying the course and the expanse of a movement in the market. This tactic is completely foreign to the average investor or trader.

There will be an effort to educate the reader to partially divulge still other mathematical distant ideas behind the stock and futures market when it is allowable in the book. The main objective of the book is to train the readers mind to understand the narrowly defined area of the subject matter of ellipses and pattern charts. The methods and rules used in the book will be based on sound fundamental laws of nature using market trading tactics.

This book will strive to unlock the principal laws of movement of the markets.

Larry Jacobs

IDEALISTIC PERCEPTIONS

Day after day we visualize pictures and objects in our mind. We draw on these objects from everyday images, which we see and are absorbed in our mind and applied to our everyday activities. Instinctively we ascertain these images in our mind so that we might draw conclusions as to what they make up and how they can be used in our interaction with our daily activities.

Depending on our individual ability and wholehearted observation we can move forward to a higher level of the science of visualizing images from recurring study of them. Some people might call this practical experience. This practical experience must be combined with thought to elevate the student to a higher and keener level of expertise of recognizing objects. The more experience an person has in recognizing objects and analyzing them, the more he is apt to be successful in this endeavor.

It's almost impossible to visualize a car traveling on the highway upside down. Your past experience of seeing or driving a car has convinced you that it is impossible for a car to travel upside down, except for the possible exception of it being turned over in a moving accident.

Similar comparisons can be made is visualizing other objects and there movements. Your past experience causes your mind to restrain your ability to mentally picture hypothetical images.

In this book the reader will be taught to recognize images of patterns and ellipses and how they can be used to detect changes of trends. It is extremely important that the reader allows his mind to fully develop in this area. This can only be done with extensive study and visualizing these patterns and ellipses on a continuing basis. Repetition is the name of the game. The more you do it, the better you will get at it.

The trader must pay attention to the market. He must know when to buy and sell by watching the market's stop and go signals.

Patterns and Ellipses

Psychology plays an important part in the profits and loses of a trader. If a trader buys a security when the market is in a downtrend and experiences a loss, he must learn from it and not do the same mistake again. The pattern he visualized was incorrect and he must analyze what went wrong and not do it again. Some traders are stubborn and feel the market cheated them and they'll get their money back next time using the same signal and doubling up. The trader did not watch the stoplight. The same patterns occur over and over again. The trader will only begin to be successful when he starts to pay attention and remembers the patterns whatever they may be.

Larry Jacobs

WHAT IS IMPLIED BY TIME?

Things subsist or events come about because we know what has happened in the past. What is and what exists only because of their connection with other things or what other things have happened. Therefore everything that exists or happens is then in someway connected to everything else that has exists or has happened. This is an endless sequence to infinity.

What is duration? It's the lapse of time between the launching of an event and the termination of the event. This duration is therefore called time as we know it. Time is as we understand it, is a line from the present that extends itself to an end in the future. As time progresses each present moment becomes part of the past. The future never ends as time continues to roll steadily forward. Imagine in your mind's eye a river flowing from a far-away past into an endless future.

Visualizing an abstract river does not bring us anything helpful. Nothing is achieved if an abstract picture is substituted for a time line. Everything that happens occurs in connection with something else. Time is as the crow flies, a straight line. The flow of time does not carry events and happenings with it. Events and happenings rather occur with or along the path of time.

Much discussion could be developed along this line of thinking. We would ultimately arrive again at our beginning line of thought.

Herein this book lies a possible explanation of the concept of time and how to apply it to trading the markets. W.D. Gann said in analyzing the markets, time is the most important factor. It doesn't really matter where a trader buys or sells a stock or futures contract, but rather when. It the trader buys and market time is moving up, he will make move. If the trader shorts and market time is moving down then the trader will make money. It's not important that a trader buys the exact bottom and sells at the exact top. Only idiots say they bought the exact bottom or sold at the exact top. It doesn't really matter. All that does matter is the profit

Patterns and Ellipses

is made on the transaction.

Larry Jacobs

THE RULES OF TIME

Time falls into the formation of nature and substance. The following are the rules of time:

1) The universe is infinite and unlimited in matter.

2) Time is unlimited and has no beginning and is without end.

3) Matter is everywhere and it's in constant motion.

4) The universe's motion is circular.

Copernicus, a famous astrologer, announced a long time ago that the Earth rotated around the Sun. This was directly contrasting all the previous views that the Sun rotated around the Earth.

Since the universe's motion is circular, time and the universe affects time, it stands to reason that time's straight line in therefore affected by the circulation motion of the universe.

Patterns and Ellipses

MOVEMENT IN THE UNIVERSE

Anybody that has movement in the universe has the tendency by natural law to keep moving in a straight line until something interferes with that movement and compels it to change.

When my grandfather was a young man, there was a national contest in the United States to develop a perpetual motion machine. That's a machine that would continue to move once started until infinity. He worked on his machine for months and months, just to find out that it was impossible. His machine and everyone else's failed due to friction and gravity. The law of nature is that everything in motion is subject to natural decay unless some additional energy is given to the object from time to time. It is therefore impossible to create a mechanism that will produce surplus energy, which would make it possible to stay continuously in motion.

When we construct a chart of a stock or futures contract we also become conscious of the fact that like laws are in force. The figure below shows daily chart Dupont. Something caused the stock to decline at point A down in to B. At B something major caused the stock to take off and move quickly. The movement slowed at point C where it declined into point D and up into point E where their was a complete loss of motion. It then had a sharp drop into F. It recovered back up into G and back down again into H. Something new then caused the stock to move up sharply from H. See the chart below.

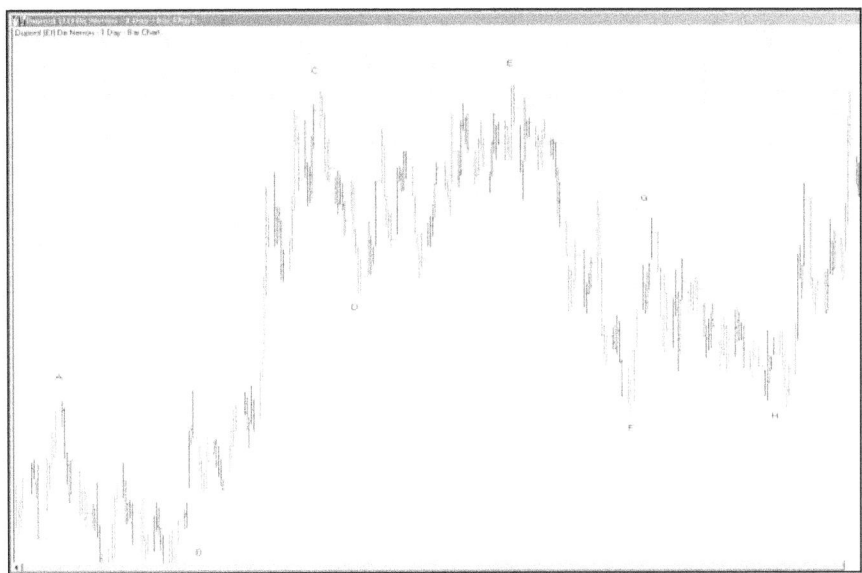

The free will choice of man, which causes him to buy and sell at different time periods in the stock, was the underlying reason why it moved. Buying and selling pressure is what causes the market to move. The will of the majority of traders who make their decisions on their own or being advised by television or advisors is moves the market.

The universe is a well-arranged body and all the objects in it provide some purpose. There is a reason for the existence of each body. Everybody in the universe in some way interacts with all other bodies in the universe. There is really no accident in the universe. Everything happens for a reason.

Let's look at all the bodies in the universe. Notice all the spherical motion of all the planets around the Sun. Our solar system is part of a much large system and it rotates around other planets and Suns. Everybody in the universe has some relation to other bodies in the universe in some way, no matter how slight.

The stock market and futures markets also have similar characteristics. For example the movement of the S&P500 Index has an effect on how the Utilities or Transportation Groups move.

Patterns and Ellipses

The Utilities has a direct Effect on a particular utility stock and to a lesser extent and effect on a Transportation Group individual stock. Even an individual stock has a slight effect on the S&P500 Index and the Utilities and Transportation Groups. The CRB Index has an effect on all Futures Groups like meats, metals, grains, foods and the like. The individual groups all have an effect on individual futures. The individual futures contracts have a slight affect on the CRB Index and the Future Groups. The CRB Index also has an effect on the S&P Index and vice versa. The seasonal weather changes have an effect on the individual futures contracts and groups and well as an impact on the S&P500 Index and stock categories and individual stocks. Everything in the markets is in some way directly or indirectly related to everything else in a gigantic circle of movement. The smallest of these circles is related to the larger circles of movement and progressive growth. The bigger circles have more impact than the smaller circles. Every market in some way acts like a wheel of another wheel. See the following chart.

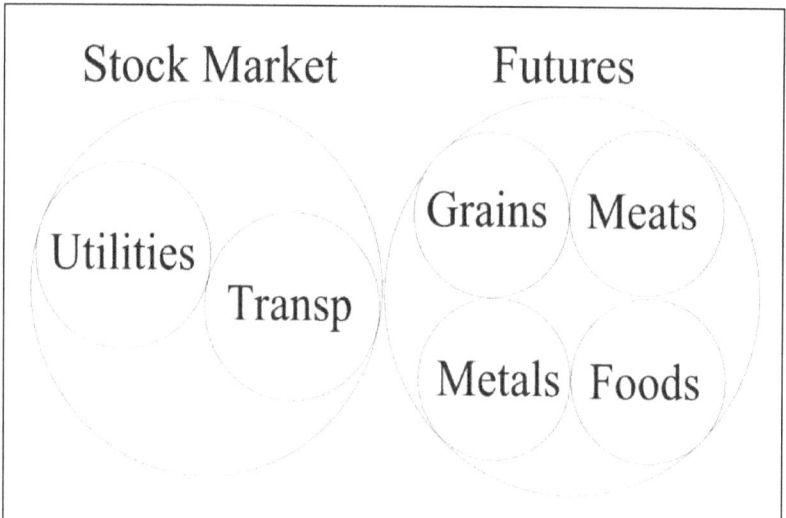

The diagram only represents a small part of the number of circles working with each other in the markets, world, planetary system and the universe. The Sun and the Moon are continually changing their motion and have the biggest impact on Earth of all the planetary bodies in our universe since the Sun is the largest body and the moon is the closest to the Earth. The Moon completes one revolution around the Earth every 27 days. The revolution of the Earth around the Sun takes 365 days. These revolutions of course give you two of the most important cycles in the markets. The passageway of the earth about the Sun is not straight to the East. It has a progress movement at the same time from South to North and from North to South, bringing about the important seasonal changes of summer and winter and fall and spring.

There are many in today's market that label planetary movement relating to cycles in the market as taboo and not any science as such. They maintain it to be impossible and more like charlatanism. They don't give it any kind of name, but just ignore it. If these people would realize that planetary movement and cycles relating to their movements are in the bible, they might change their opinion. The bible is, of course, the most studied book in the world! It's written in every tongue in the world. The bible hid the interpretation of the planets motions in stories that could be believed by everyone, wealthy or pauper, scholarly professors or non-educated people.

Planets travel in ellipses, directly akin to a circle. The circle is in actual fact an ellipse anyway. The one fact that you may not understand or know is that human too are planets of a much smaller size, but never the less influenced by the other bodies in the universe. Therefore they move in an elliptical path and are influenced by other bodies moving in their paths.

HOW THE MARKET PLACE WORKS

The NYSE and NASDAQ are organizations, which facilitates an fair and orderly regulated exchange of values of securities, stocks and bonds. The trade between the buyer and the seller is not direct, but rather it is made through the exchange that acts as an intermediary between the parties and guarantees the payment and the reception of money for securities sold. They accept no other responsibility except for the above. They buyer may be in New York and the seller in Kansas. Each pay their commission charges to brokers who act as agents for them. These brokers maintain offices for the customers to send their certificates to and to get their money and for the buyer to sent his money to and receive the certificates. Newspapers, data services and Internet sites office quotes for all transactions in the securities. Also offered are earnings and dividend reports. Many also give opinions and ratings of the securities rates. Some give buy and sell recommendations.

Generally in rough stock market times the public prefers to buy stocks that pay dividends, until the dividend is cut, and then they sell the stock. In this period of time appreciation of stocks is secondary to dividends. Dividends are most important. They feel that if they can hold a stock and it yields a decent return, they can hold it until things get better.

Also in a rough market atmosphere, the public prefers to buy long rather than to sell short. Each transaction is equal though. You can make just as much shorting a stock as buying it. Professionals tend to be more attuned to shorting than the public.

Larry Jacobs

TYPES OF PEOPLE WHO BUY AND SELL STOCK

There are several types of people who buy and sell stock. The majority of stockholders are long-term buyers. They try to buy value and hold them for long periods of time, even years. They usually never sell for several reasons. The main reason they don't sell is to avoid the tax they would have to pay. They will ride a stock from $5 to $150 and not sell for tax reasons just to have it then decline to $75.

The next type of stock buyer is the one that just buy low priced stocks. They don't determine if the stock has quality. They just want a low price stock. They feel that the market will eventually move up because it is just too low. These stocks are low for a reason. Many times these low priced stocks just go bankrupt. Occasionally one will rebound due to a fundamental development in the company.

The third type of trader buys stocks for swings in the market. This trader will hold stocks from 3 days to a month. He is generally looking for stocks that move with the trend. He buys when he thinks the price and value is low and sells when he thinks the value and price art too high. This type of trader also will have no reservation about shorting in the market since he is looking for short-term swings of any type.

The last type of is the day-trader. He watches the screen constantly and tries to make short-term profits on a few ticks or on news events. He listens to CNBC and tries to make profits on short-term pops or declines. He trades constantly and is afraid to be in the market overnight. He trades many times during the day and the commissions eat him up. The life of one of these traders is generally 3 months to 1 to 2 years, depending on how much money he has. He will usually eventually loose all of his money. These traders come and go. It's amazing, but there is always a new one of these type of traders that takes the place of one that went broke.

Patterns and Ellipses

The biggest killer of this trader is overtrading. Commissions eat him up. Also this type of trader has limited funds and has high anxiety about taking a trade overnight. He takes unusually high risks and is over margined. He'll make a short day-trade an make a fraction of a point on a stock and turn around and loose 2-3 full points on another stock, just to have the first stock he purchased make a really big move, he should have been in on.

The day-trader and the long-term buyers are the two ends of the market. Neither one of these will usually make money in the market. Also the low priced stock buyer rarely makes money, because this is a high-risk endeavor. The trader who trades the swings in the market is the one that is usually most successful, if he uses proven mathematical techniques. There are some traders that use combinations of the above methods and their success is tied to the success of the trading methodology applied to each method.

Larry Jacobs

PERSONAL FEELINGS

People who trade on personal feelings in the market usually loose their money. It's actually a personal weakness to think they can make solid buy and sell decisions based on an internal hunch. Personal opinions are not practicable for making money. Generally a person making these opinions is right only 20% of the time. Occasionally you will find a person that actually has good internal hunches that work, but they are few and far in between. These people have a gift and are usually rich and don't need anyone's advice. They usually buy massively amounts of low price stocks, which advance to high prices. These people sell at the top and reap big profits. This is an enormous gift of nature bestowed on them. Many of these people are not conscious that they even have this gift.

Every single trader and investor needs to have solid advice or base his decisions upon mathematical laws of trading. Experience with solid mathematical laws is the secret to success in the market.

OVERTRADING

Overtrading as stated earlier is the biggest weakness you can have in the market. This has bankrupt more traders in the markets than any other reason. Overtrading can take many forms. The first form of overtrading is when a trader over margins his stock. When a downturn comes it wipes the trader out with just a small move against him in the markets. He then has to liquidate his positions before the market can recover. Fully margining is especially dangerous in very volatile stocks with large swings.

Another form of overtrading is buying too large number of stocks to be able to effectively follow. The trader spreads himself too thin, where he can't keep track of all of his holdings. It's better to put your money in a handful of high quality stocks than in 20 to 30 unknown stocks that you can't follow closely.

Of course, the biggest form of overtrading is just making too many trades during the day. Also this excessive day trading causes the trader to take small profits of less than 1 point and large losses of 2 to 3 points. These large loses eventually eat up most of his capital and the remainder is eaten up by commissions.

Larry Jacobs

HOW DO YOU KNOW WHAT THE MARKET WILL DO TOMORROW?

The biggest question in every investor's mind is what will the market do tomorrow, next week, next month or even next year. How can one arrange his investments to take advantage of this market? If you watch and listen to the CNBC television network, you will find that these are the two questions that are asked almost every person being interviewed.

It's a tragedy that most new people entering the market with tremendous enthusiasm and high spirits will fail. They have many ideas on how to make money in the markets and to achieve higher returns than other traders. Most of them, unfortunately, lose all of their money. Some of them return again, with new fresh capital, just to again lose it all.

There are a few traders spend the time and effort to study the mathematics behind the market and to learn trading techniques before they trade. They develop a trading methodology and fully back test it using historical data. When they are ready they apply the trading techniques to the market with money management and they succeed. These are extremely disciplined traders. These traders know how succeed and they are equipped with the right tools. These traders know that there is no scheme in trading the market that works all of the time. Sometimes traders lose, but they cut their losses short when they are in a loosing trade and when they are in a winning trade, they let their profits go. They realize that day trading in the end usually produces losses and the only way they are going to make big money is to let their profits run and protect themselves with stops.

Patterns and Ellipses

Larry Jacobs

LAWS OF THE MARKET

There is no system in the market, which works all the time. The small intraday minor trades are all part of the big larger moves. These represent smaller cycles working in larger cycles or small wheels working in larger wheels. The time and effort that must be expended on these small moves is usually not worth it and wears out the trader. When he is worn out, he usually misses the big moves. The time required to find moves of an hour or two usually take the same amount of time to find bigger moves. These small jiggles of the market should usually be avoided. You should then avoid buying in the morning and selling before the close. Rather you should buy sometime in the day knowing that the trend is upward and that will last several days and approximately when and where it will end.

Time laws should be the primary focus of your trading rather than price laws. As W. D. Gann said, time is the most important factor. It doesn't matter if the price is at the low when you buy, but only that it starts moving up after you buy.

METHODS OF BUYING

To be a better trader it's necessary that you understand the methods of buying people use. The first method used is investors that buy stocks based on earnings, dividends and the outlook of the finances of a company. This is the method used by most brokerage firms to promote their research department. This type of investing is called the fundamental approach. In most cases this information is past history. By the time a research report comes out telling clients that a firm does not look good in the way of sales, earning and dividends, it's already too late. The price of the company's stock has already taken a big drop. These research reports merely explain what has already happened in the past and has no bearing on the future of the company. Most of the time this group of buyers is completely lost. If a stock drops when good news comes out, they can't explain it. If a stock rises with bad earning, they can't explain it. This group of traders and investors is living in the past and not in the future.

The second method of buying is buying the good news on a stock. These people tend to watch CNBC all day on television. They have their eyes are glued on the ticker. They even eat lunch watching the various CNBC programs, hoping they won't miss something important. They are constantly overwhelmed with news and interviews from company officials. Investment advisors are constantly telling them how and what to invest in. It's not possible for them to comprehend all the news they are getting. These people frequently lose their perspective and capabilities of making good decisions. When the stocks they buy start to decline, there is no one to give them an opinion as to what to do. They are constantly in the state of confusion.

The third method of buying is with charts. They follow the charts using the available oscillators on their computer. They are constantly listing to the leading news stories. They spend very little time understanding or researching the technical methods of trading they use, but are in it for the thrill it gives them.

The fourth type is the group that develops and back-tests technical trading methods. When they are confident and have seen it work a sufficient number of times they test it on the market. They then trade the market very carefully and use protective stops.

KNOW YOUR STOCKS

You should try to trade in stocks that you know and that you have made money with before. Avoid those stocks that you have lost money in before. Don't ever try to get even with a stock that you have lost money on. Usually that stock will get more of your money. The problem is that your vibrations are not in sync with that stock.

You should never buy a stock or commodity on a hunch or on the idea of someone else who has no knowledge or who is not qualified to make quality-buying suggestions. You should only do buying when many factors come together that you are watching. Until that happens take your time and be careful. You must put together all of the factors that you think are reasons to buy and weight them carefully and then make the purchase and use stops and let nature take it course.

Always use sufficient market to trade with. Using thin margins will usually disturb your free and clear thought. If you have made a slight error in your calculations to buy, you might need to withstand the market going against you until the trend turns in your direction.

Larry Jacobs

KNOW THE TYPES OF CHARTS TO USE

There are now several types of charts to use. The bars in the following examples are color-coded. This is a black & white book therefore you won't see the colors. You do have the ability to view a 30-trial of the Market-Analyst software in the back of this book. With this software you can view the colors on your computer color screen. Now here are the types of charts:

Patterns and Ellipses

BAR CHART TIME SEPARATION

This is an excellent Gann style of bar chart. It uses normal open, high, low close charts. The bars are color-coded. When the bar makes a higher high the color turns blue, when the bar makes a lower low the color turns green.

BAR CHART – STENGTH

This is also another type of regular bar chart based on strength or momentum. When the bar is strong its color is blue and when it's weak the color is red.

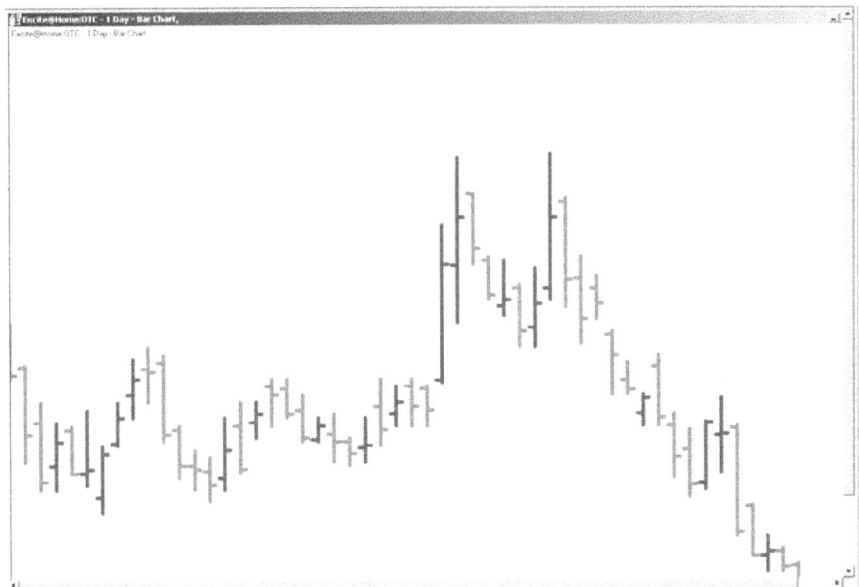

Patterns and Ellipses

BAR CHART - SWING

This type of bar chart is green when it makes a higher high, neural when it is an inside bar, black when it's an outside bar and red when it makes a lower low. Remember that both inside and outside bars many times indicate a short-term change of trend in the market.

Larry Jacobs

CANDLESTICK CHARTS

This is a special type of chart in which each bar can give you a different signal from its formation. Candlestick Charts are a variation of the Bar Chart used to visually search for various patterns in the market. A Candlestick Chart is similar to a Bar Chart except that the open and close are used to determine where the rectangles are being drawn. The position of the close, relative to the open, determines whether the Candle is solid or a wire frame. There are entire books written on the subject of trading these types of charts.

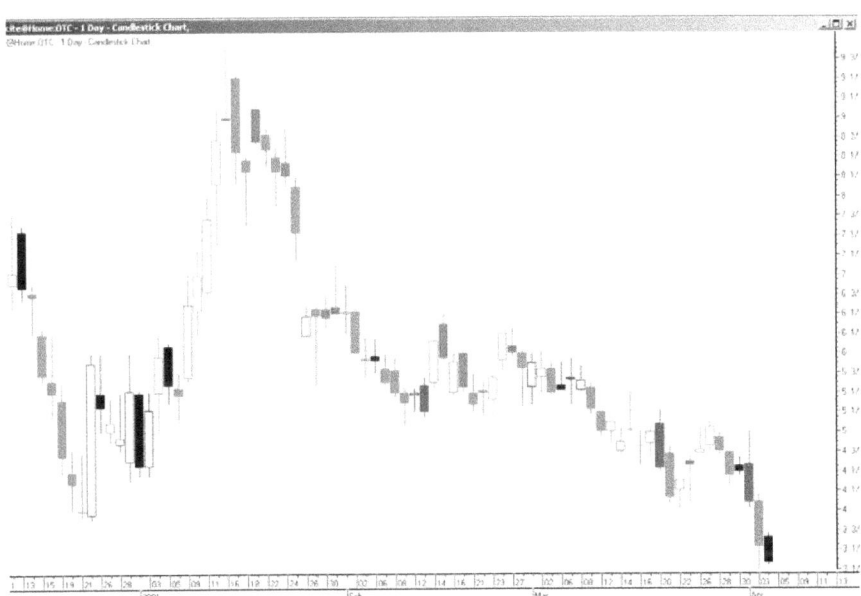

Patterns and Ellipses

GANN SWING BAR CHART

The Swing Chart takes the time element out of the bar chart and represents only the movement of the price.

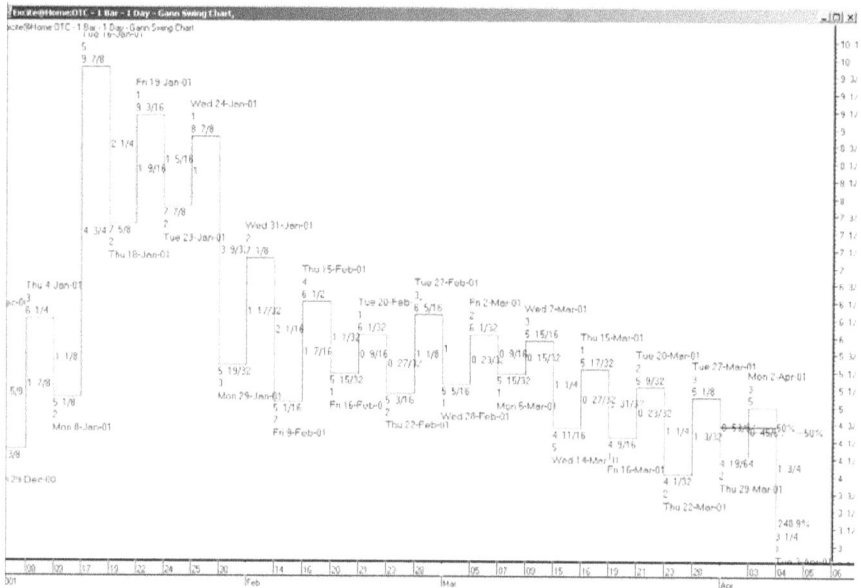

The figures on the Swing Chart provide valuable information. The figures at each end of a swing are the date of the change in the swing, the number of bars that make up the swing, and the price that the swing turned. The number in the middle of the swing is the range of the swing. Swing Bars. Sets how many bars must be in the same direction for the swing to turn. For example, if set to three, there would have to be three successive higher bars before a down swing would turn up.

* Outside Bar Method. Select how outside bars are handled.

* Label Font. This option allows you to set the size, style, and color of the font that is used to display the swing figures on the chart.

* Use Inside Days. If this option is checked, then Inside Bars are used in counting swings. Otherwise they are ignored.

* Display Prices. If this option is checked, then details regarding the swings will be displayed on the Swing Chart.

* Show 50% Line. This option allows you to display two 50% horizontal lines on the last two swings of the chart.

Patterns and Ellipses

SWING CHART IMPOSED ON REGULAR BAR CHART

Swing charts produce rising and falling lines to indicate price movement with the time element removed. For a swing to turn up, the market must have one higher bar. (A higher bar is one where the top of the bar is higher than the previous bar, and the low is higher than the previous bar.) For a swing to turn down, the market must have a lower bar (Lower top, and lower bottom than the previous bar).

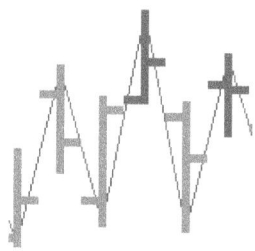

1 Bar Swing Chart

In the image above, the swing is initially moving up. The lower bar makes the swing turn down. The next bar is a higher bar and the swing moves up again and so on.

Multiple Bar Swing Charts

As a one bar swing chart can move up and down very rapidly it is considered too noisy to make any judgment on trend. The most common practice to filter out the noise of a swing chart is to specify a given number of bars in any direction to change the swing. For example, in a 3 bar swing chart, if a swing is moving down, it will require 3 higher bars before the swing will turn up.

Larry Jacobs

3 Bar Swing Chart

In this example, the swing is initially moving up. The occurrence of five lower bars turns the swing down. The next two bars are higher bars, but as they are only two higher bars, the swing stays down.

Outside Bars

The examples so far have been based on bars, which have higher and lower tops and bottoms. An outside bar is one, which has a higher top and a lower bottom than the previous bar. Market Analyst gives you the option as to how you deal with outside bars.

The first method, use next bar, waits until the bar following the outside bar is received, then the swing is processed. If the swing is moving down and the bar after the outside bar is higher, then the swing would continue to the bottom of the outside bar and then turn to the top of the following bar. If the swing is moving down and the bar after the outside bar is a lower bar, then the swing would turn to the top of the outside bar and then turn again to the bottom of the following bar.

The second method is use outside Bar. In this method the swing is calculated using the position of the open and close of the outside bar itself. If a swing is moving down and the open is lower than the close, then the swing would continue to the bottom of the outside bar and then turn to the top of the outside bar. If the swing is moving down and the open is higher than the close, then the swing

Patterns and Ellipses

would turn to the top of the outside bar and then turn again to the bottom of the outside bar.

Inside Bars

Inside bars are bars that have their high price lower than the previous bar and the low price higher than the previous bar. In Market Analyst there is an option to include inside bars in swing chart creation. This only applies where the swing requires multiple higher or lower bars to turn. In a three bar swing chart a swing requires an inside bar and two higher or lower bars to turn. Inside bars are generally ignored in calculating swings.

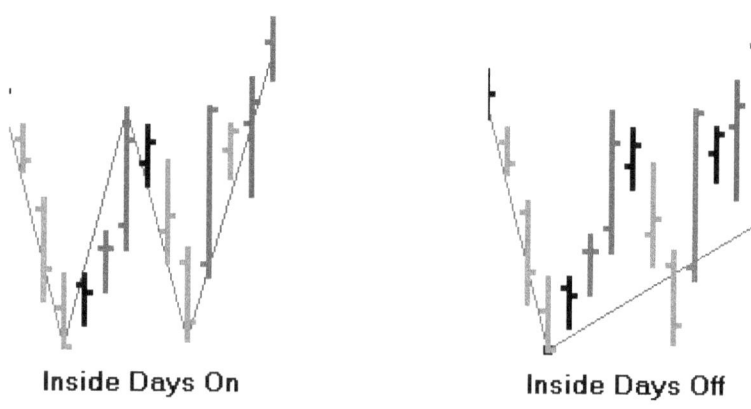

Inside Days On   **Inside Days Off**

The images above, taken from the same position in a 3 bar swing chart, show the swing when the "use inside days" option is turned on and off.

Exceptions

There are a few exceptions in calculating swings. If a market gaps and there is a bar lower than the previous swing bottom, or higher than the previous swing top, the swing will turn even if the required number of bars has not been reached.

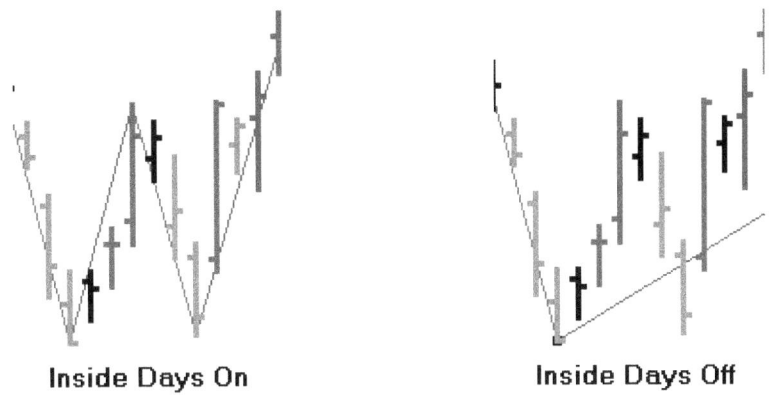

Inside Days On   Inside Days Off

In this example, the 3 bar swing chart is moving up and would normally require three bars to turn down. As the lower bar is lower than the previous swing bottom, the swing turned without waiting for the second and third bar.

In the following example we set up a chart with 3 minimum bars per swing. We also included ellipses for direction and used outside bar signals to buy the bottoms of ellipses.

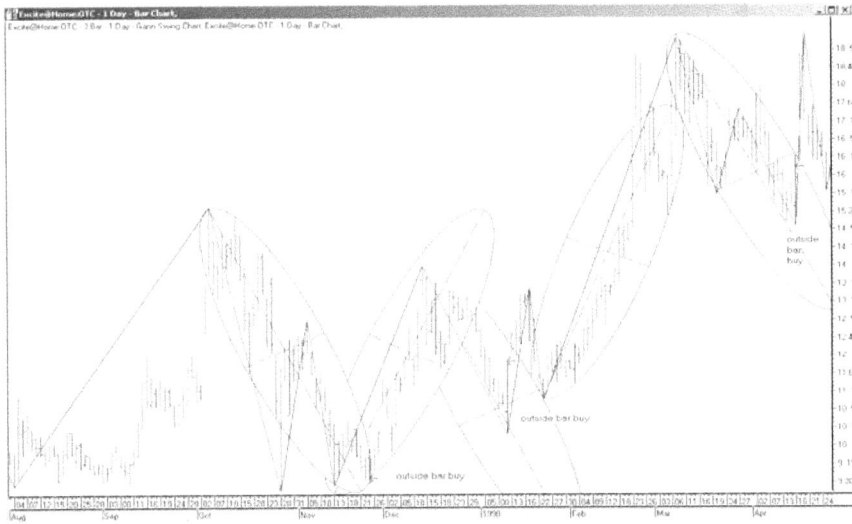

Patterns and Ellipses

GANN SWING CHART

The following chart illustrated a 1-point Gann Swing chart. That means the market has to move through the prior day's low or high by one point to change the swing direction of the market. After the swing changes direction its best to let the market makes its first reaction then either buy or sell into the trend. These kinds of charts can be experimented with and the swing numbers can be changed.

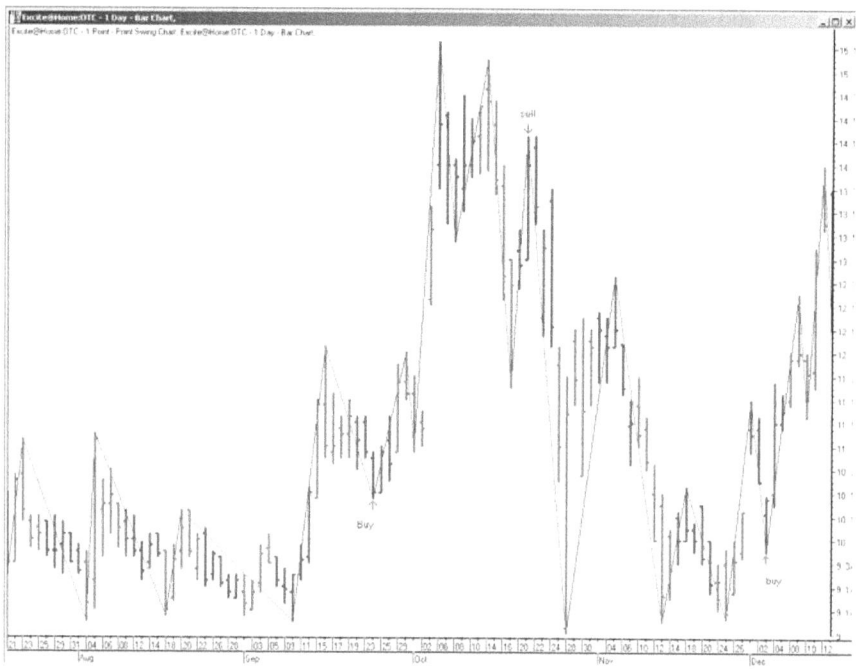

Larry Jacobs

BARROS SWINGS

The Barros Swing is a trend indicator and can be used much like Gann Swings. Ray Barros developed this method for successful trading. The Swing method uses three different time frames, short, intermediate and long term for trading signals. The best technique for successful trades is the make sure both the long term and intermediate swings are in your direction and take a short-term swing in the direction of the other two.

In the example below all three swings, long-term, intermediate-term and short-term went long December 22 when they all turned up. The market then took off and broke into new highs.

Patterns and Ellipses

LINE CHARTS

Line Charts are a simple way to remove the "clutter" and simply see a line joining the close of each bar. Many Elliott wave traders use line charts so they can more easily see the waves. They are especially fond of 30 minute bar charts, which show the most minute Elliott Wave patterns.

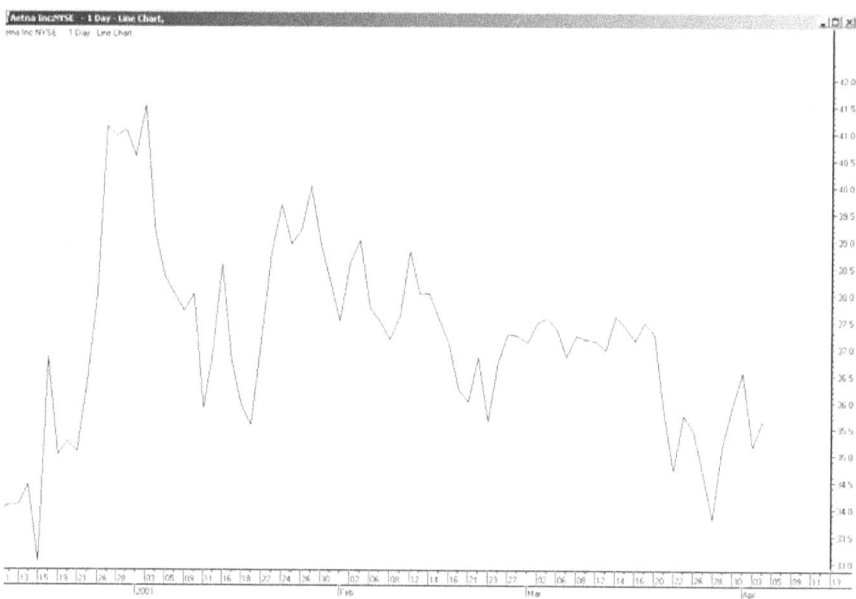

RANGE CHARTS

Range Charts provide an alternative view of the market by adjusting the width of each bar to a proportion of the range of the bar.

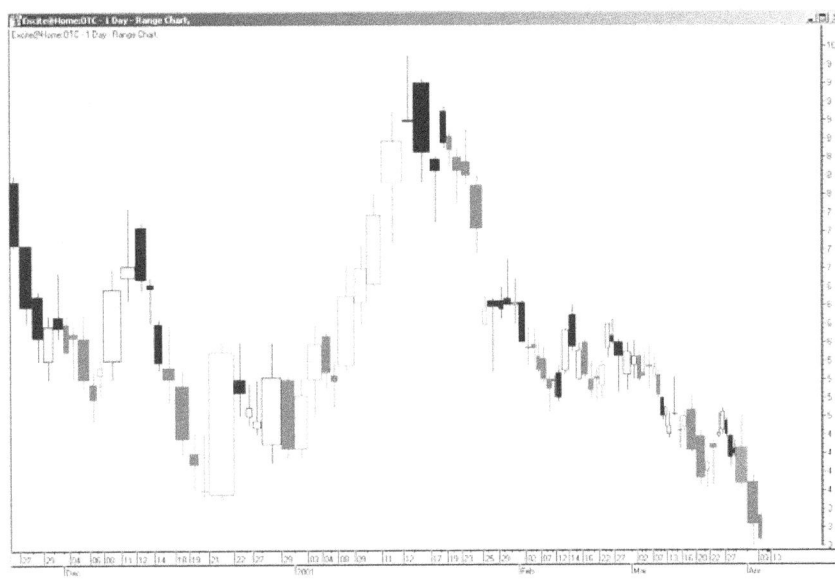

Range charts used with preset Gann angles works nicely. Time is adjusted to price with the range of the day calculated into bar width.

Patterns and Ellipses

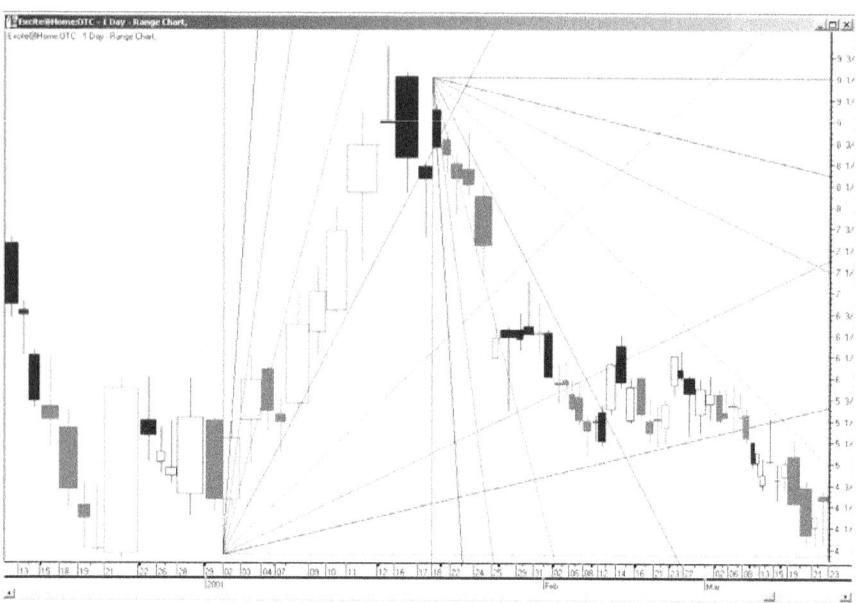

Larry Jacobs

POINT AND FIGURE CHARTS

Point and Figure Charts are another alternative chart for viewing the price movement of the market. Point and Figure charts use crosses to represent rising markets, and circles to represent falling markets. The Point & Figure Chart is similar to a Swing Chart in that it does not give an indication to time, simply the movement of price. Market Analyst adopts the standard of displaying a cross over a circle when there is only one box in either direction. The image below shows how this is represented.

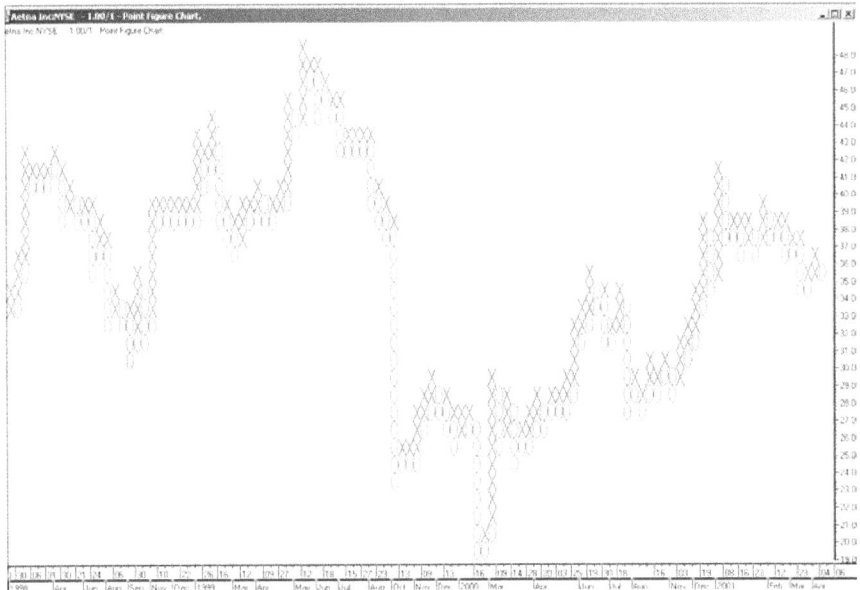

* Box Size. This option specifies the size of the each of the circles and crosses in points.

* Reverse Count. This option specifies how many boxes (circles or crosses) must be formed in the opposite direction to the market before being displayed. For example, if this is set to three and the box size is set to 10, there will have to be a 30 point move in the market before the Point & Figure Chart changes.

Patterns and Ellipses

* Label Font. This option allows you to set the size, style, and color of the font that is used to display information on the chart.

* Display Prices. If this option is selected, then details regarding the chart will be displayed on the chart.

Larry Jacobs

KAGI SWING CHART

Kagi charts were created around 1870's in Japan. Kagi charts, as with Gann Swing charts, display rising and falling vertical lines to indicate price action while ignoring the time element. The lines created by Kagi charts are usually displayed as thick or thin depending on price action, direction and the point at which prices penetrate a previous high or low. Market Analyst, however, distinguishes between the thick and thin lines using color. Green represents thick lines and red represents thin lines as the default colors.

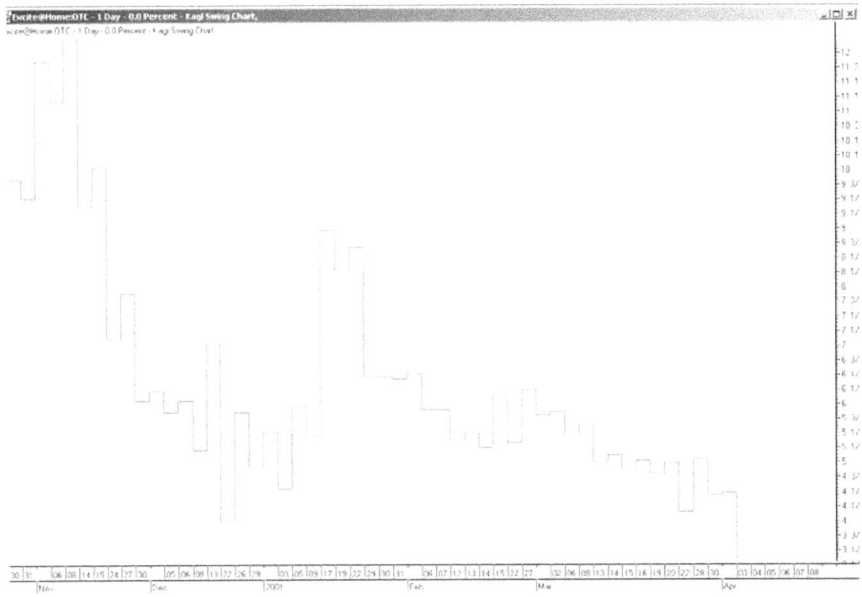

Patterns and Ellipses

CALENDAR DAYS VS TRADING DAYS

The first chart has all calendar days showing verses the second chart that shows only trading days. For time calculations it is recommended that calendar days be showing. Time continues even though the market is closed. Use both types of charts and determine which works best with the market you are using.

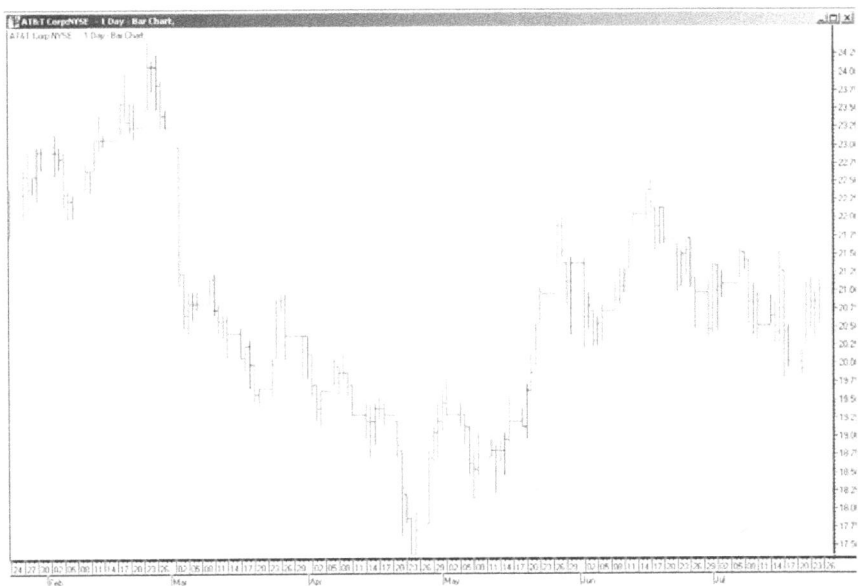

Patterns and Ellipses

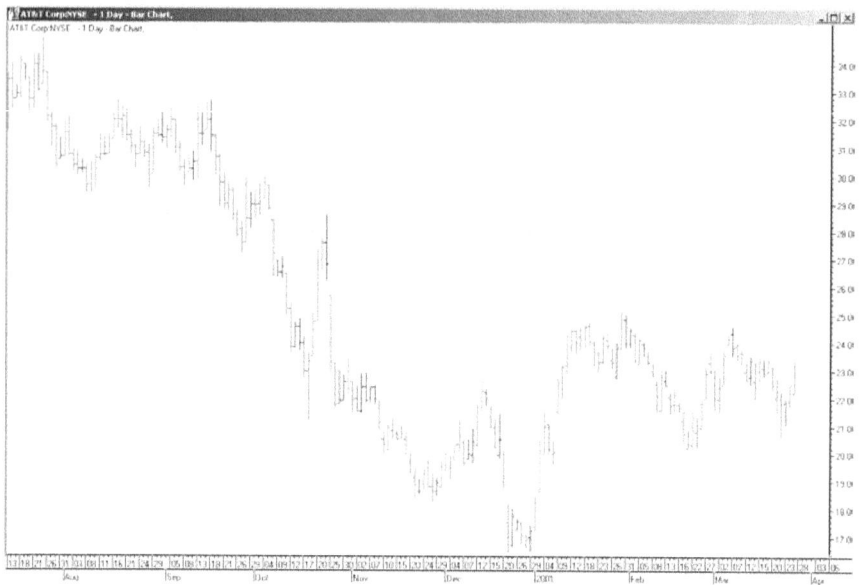

Larry Jacobs

GANN FAN ON CALENDAR BASED CHARTS

The Gann Fan is a traditional method of squaring time and price. A one-by-one line (1x1) refers to a line where every movement in time of one bar means the line will go up by one point in price value.

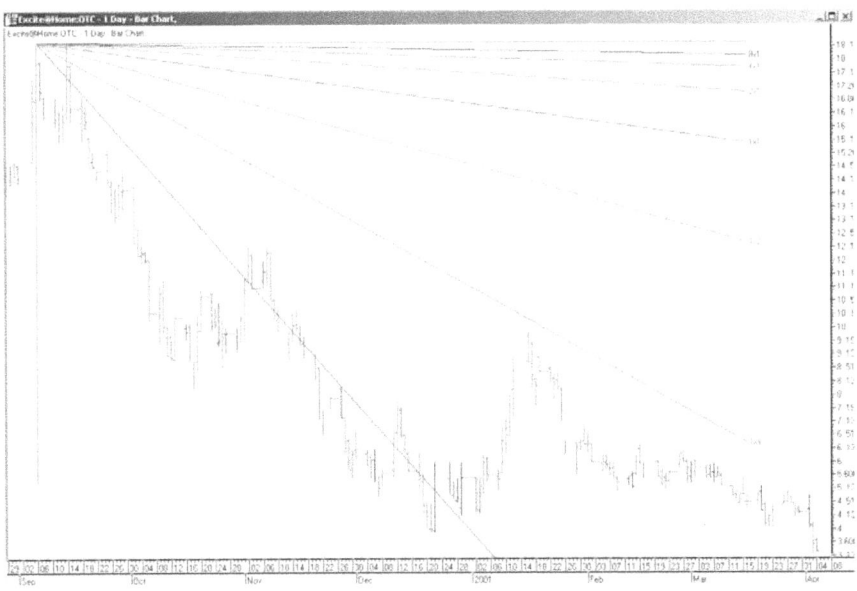

It's extremely important that Gann Fan lines be drawn correctly. Originally Gann set the angles up on K&E chart paper. The angles are really percentage divisions. If you are using a computer program to draw the angles then they should be stored as percentages. Therefore a traditional 45° line, or a one-by-one, is considered to be a value of 100%. A two-by-one, where for every one unit in time the price will increase by two, is represented by a 200% value; a three-by-one, represented by 300%, etc. A one-by-two line, where for every two periods in time the value in price only increases by one value, is depicted by 50%. A one-by-four line would be depicted as 25%.

If the Gann Fan is used on a trading day chart and a calendar day

Patterns and Ellipses

chart it's going to tell you two different things. The angles won't hit the same place. The following is the same Gann Fan drawn on a bar chart without holidays and weekends as above.

Larry Jacobs

GANN FAN ON TRADING DAY BASED CHARTS

A good program will allow you to draw the Gann Fan lines based on either calendar days or market days. It should also have an option that tells you what one unit of price is. If the chart were measured in quarters, then this value would be .25. You should also have an option of altering the percentage ratios.

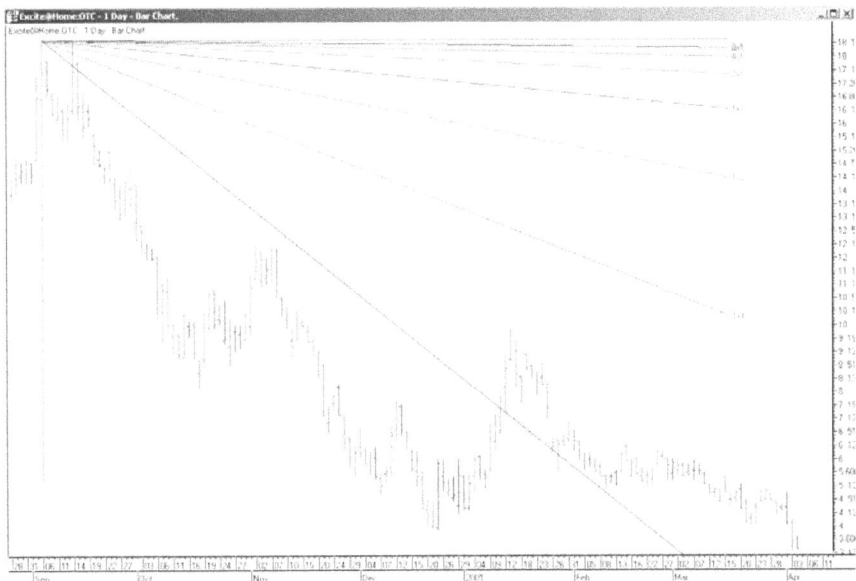

Patterns and Ellipses

GANN FAN ON CALENDAR BASED CHARTS WITH REACTIONS

How to you determine which type of chart to use with the Gann Fan lines? The best way is called best fit. Use the way that fits the chart the best. See now the calendar based chart with more angles on it.

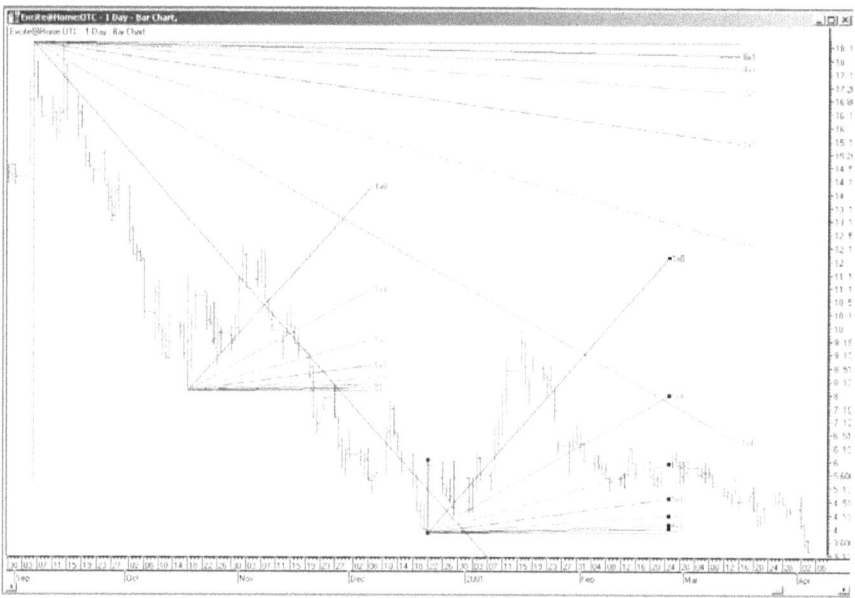

GANN FAN ON TRADING DAY BASED CHARTS WITH REACTIONS

Now look at the next trading bar based chart. The new angles drawn on it fit much better.

With this kind of chart you can have a trading strategy with. Use the main angles down for the main trend. Short the market when a 1 x 1 angle is broken. The first profit objective can be the bottom of the reaction angles.

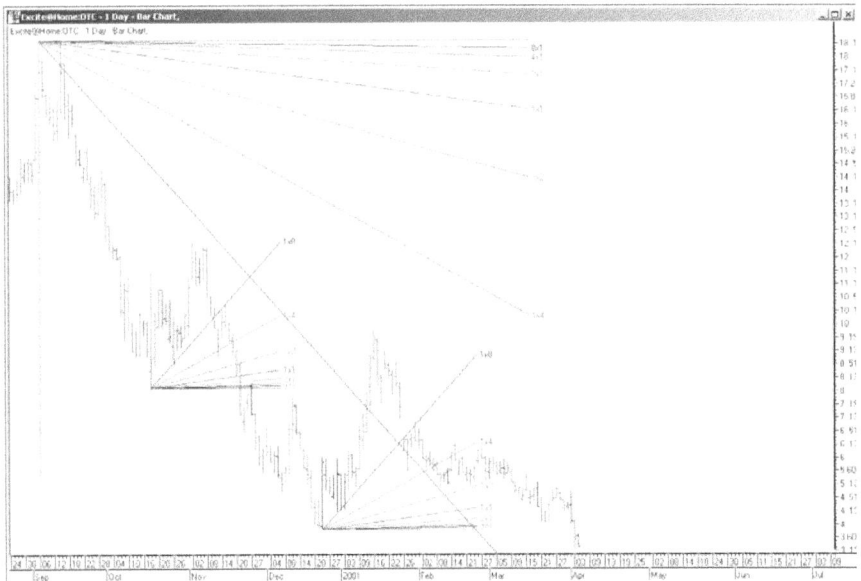

Patterns and Ellipses

USING THE GANN FAN WITH ASTROLOGY

In this example we show how you can use a reverse Gann Fan angle off of three prior lows. Projecting to a planetary aspect day of the Sun-Earth 180? Opposition. The two angles clearly gave the high and low of that day.

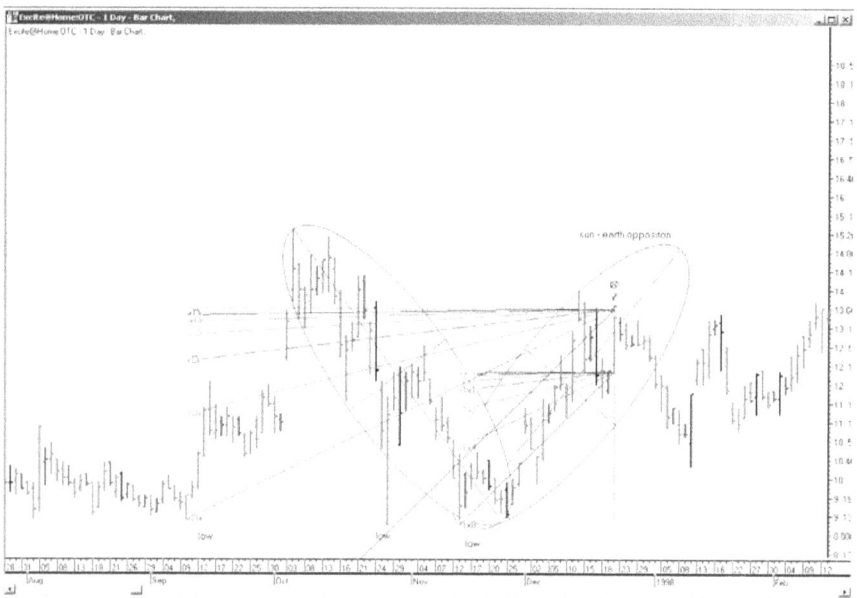

Larry Jacobs

ZERO POINT – WEEKLY CHARTS ON DEC OATS

The following illustrates taking the Gann angle off of the zero point on December Oats. Notice how nicely the angles fit the price and how the market crosses the angle lines just to go to the next angle.

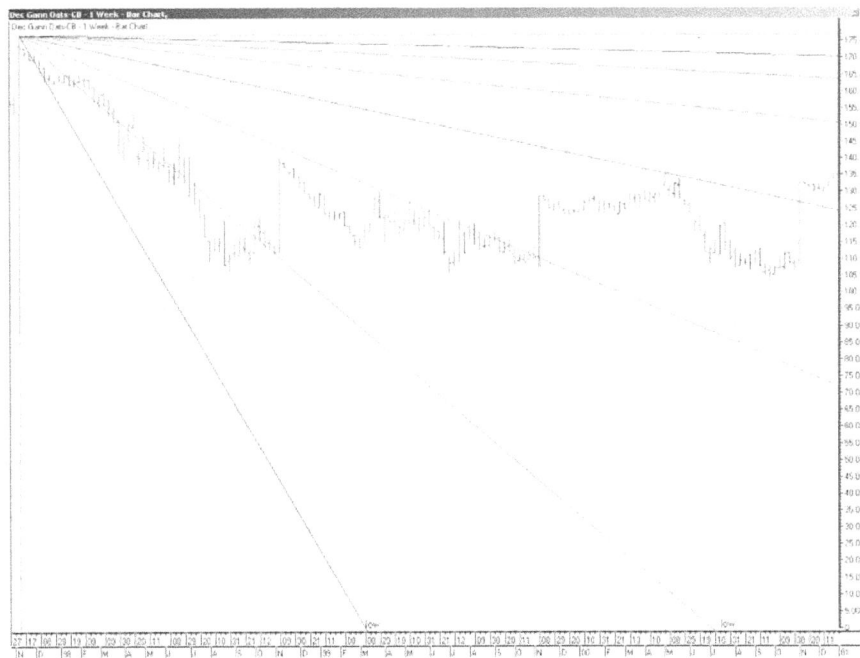

Patterns and Ellipses

SQUARING RANGE – MONTHLY CHART ON DEC COCOA

The following chart illustrates squaring the range on the monthly chart on December Cocoa. You must find the key angle that the market is working on. Sometimes it might be the 1 x 1, the 1 x 2 might be the relevant angle or even the 1 x 4 might be the key angle. A lot has to do with the scaling of the charts. In this example it's the blue angle, which intersects with the top horizontal line. When this happens the market squares itself and the market reverses its trend.

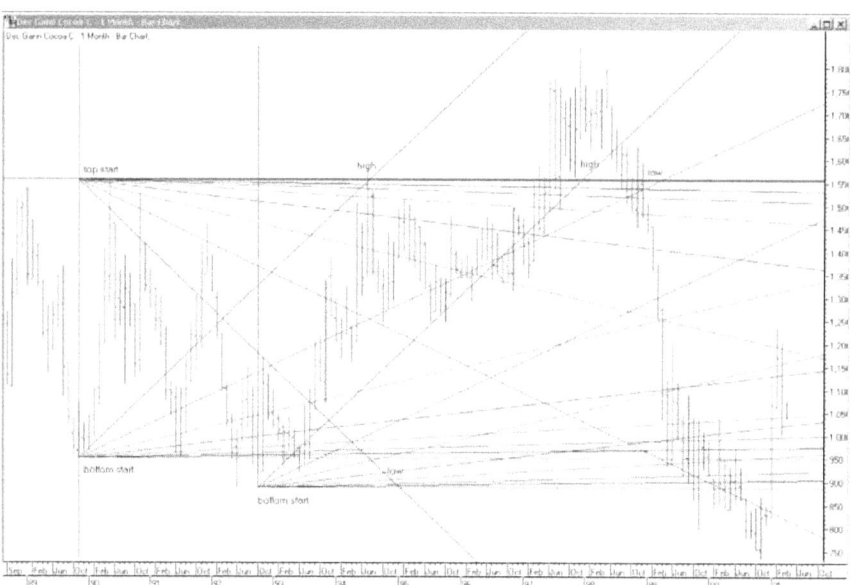

Larry Jacobs

GANN FAN GEOMETRIC ANGLES

The Advanced Gann Fan (AGF) creates fans (lines) using defined angles based on two selected points on a chart. The lines produced provide excellent support and resistance and time lines that can be extended well into the future. The Standard Gann Fan is calculated by squaring time and price. A 1x1 line has the same time division as the price division. If a security price rises by 10 units, the time division will also increase by 10 units. The AGF is purely a geometric fan where geometric angles are drawn from the starting point, the ending point, and the midpoint of a line that the user draws. See in the following example how the lines created gave trend line support and resistance. The intersecting points gave highs or lows on the chart. This is a weekly chart of the stock Excite.

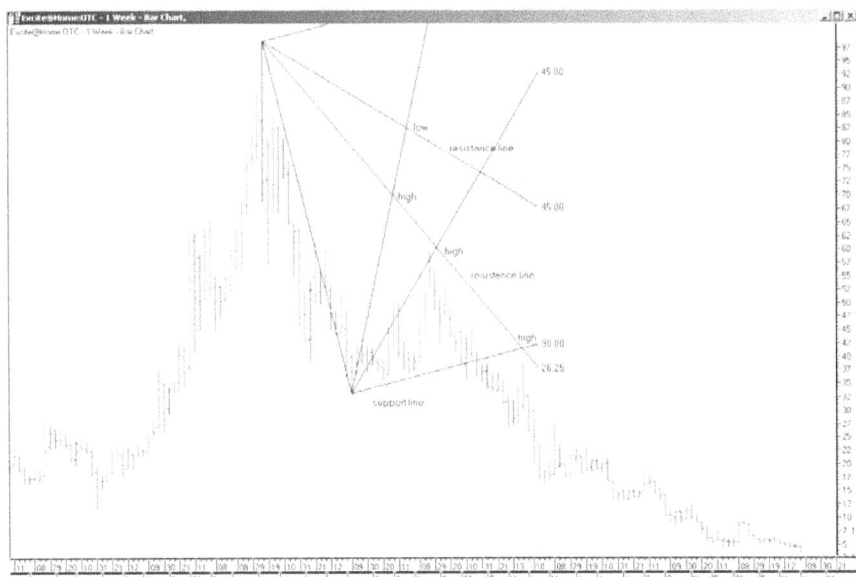

Patterns and Ellipses

Larry Jacobs

GANN SQUARES

Gann often talked about the importance of squaring time and price. The GS is a simple way of achieving this. These squares are often referred to as the square of 90, or square of 144. The time period can be calculated using bars or calendar days. The square can be divided using 1/8, 1/16, 1/4, or 1/3 lines. In this case we used 1/3 lines. Notice how these division lines of horizontal support and resistance work. Also notice has the angles work in this square. The GS is filled with a host of angles joining the various corners and midpoints of the box. Gann placed great importance on these angles. In the below example we kept the square proportionate that is height equal to width. The market bottomed early or squared itself. It then rallied to the end of the square. Many times a market will bottom early and it will have a Fibonacci relationship to the end of the square.

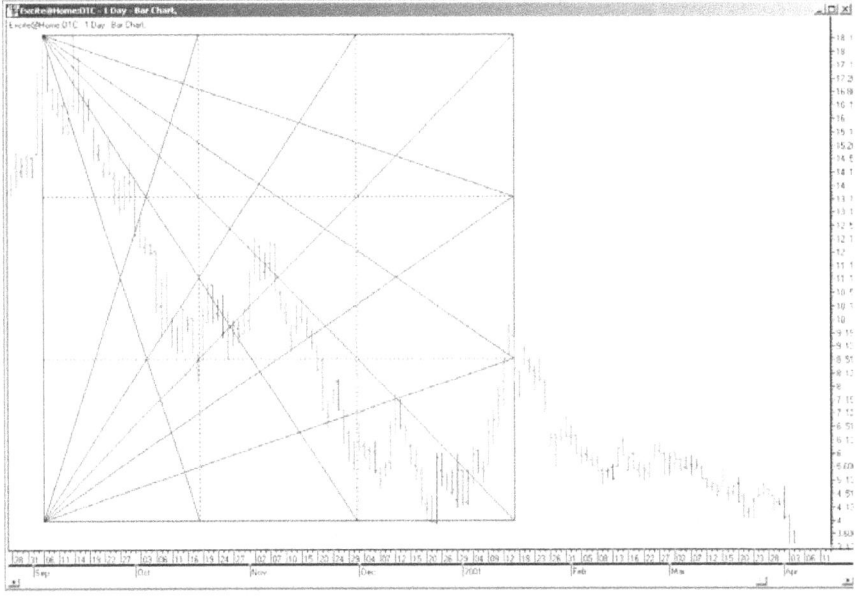

Patterns and Ellipses

Larry Jacobs

GANN SQUARES EXTENDED

Gann Square can be duplicated as many times as required in both time and price and extended into the future. The square if filled with a host of angles joining the various corners and midpoints of the box. In this example we have a Gann square of 30 extended into the future.

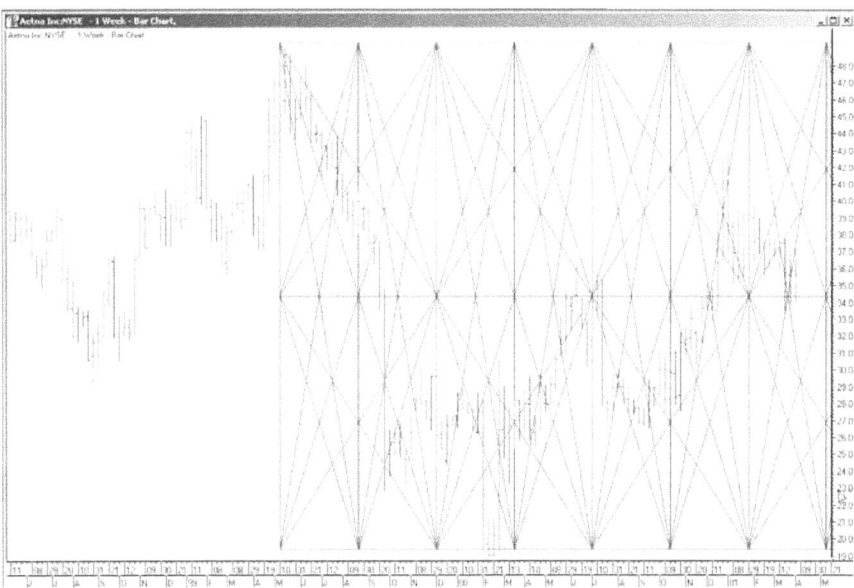

Patterns and Ellipses

THE BIBLICAL CIRCLE

According the George Bayer time is taken from the Biblical circle which is not divided by 360 degrees buy rather a little over 368 degrees. 368 divided by 3 gives us 122. Under his theory the unit of time 35 times 2.5 is then equal to 122. That means that both price and time (calendar days) move with the number of 35 in some way.

35*.25 = 8.75

35*.375= 13.125

35*.5 = 17.5

35*.625 = 21.875

35*.75 = 26.25

35*.875 = 30.625

35*1 = 35

35*2= 70

35*2.5=122

The distance between tops and bottoms in stocks and futures come out to the above numbers in many cases. See the following chart of how the stock of Dupont works inside of 72.5 and 37.5. The distance between is exactly 35. Many times the price movement starts at the first reaction as the chart below clearly shows.

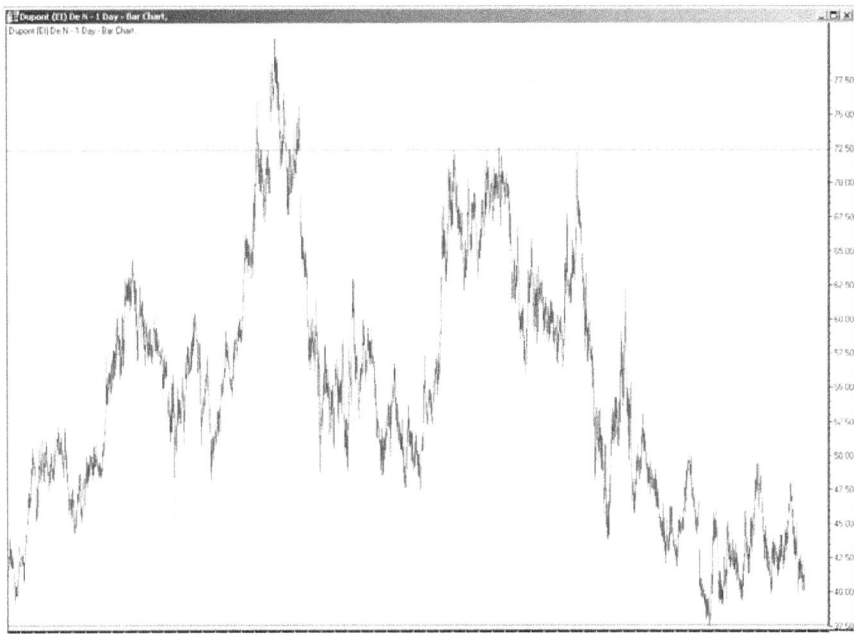

Patterns and Ellipses

35-DAY CALENDAR TIME CYCLE – DUPONT

Cycles of time also work with the same numbers. See the same chart of Dupont using the special function of a 35-day calendar time cycle.

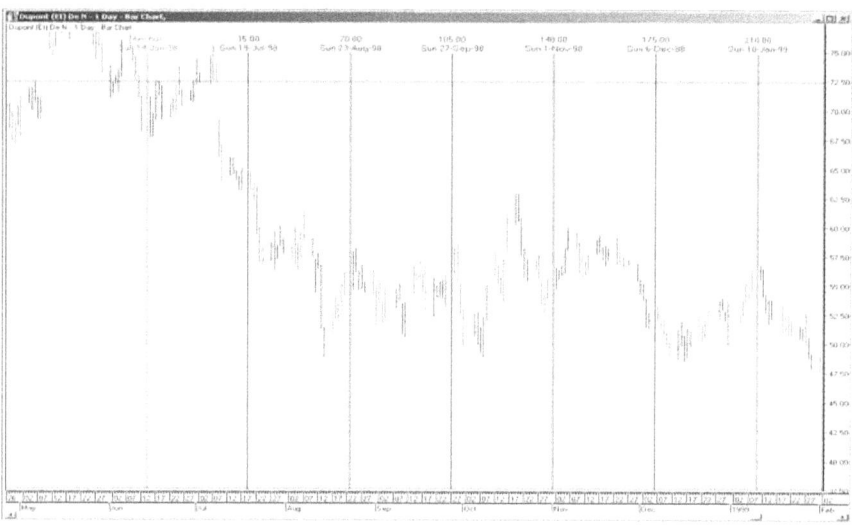

Larry Jacobs

SAME TIME COUNTS

It is possible to have several time counts at the same time starting from different beginning levels. See the following chart, Calendar Time Cycle of 35 – 2 Cycles.

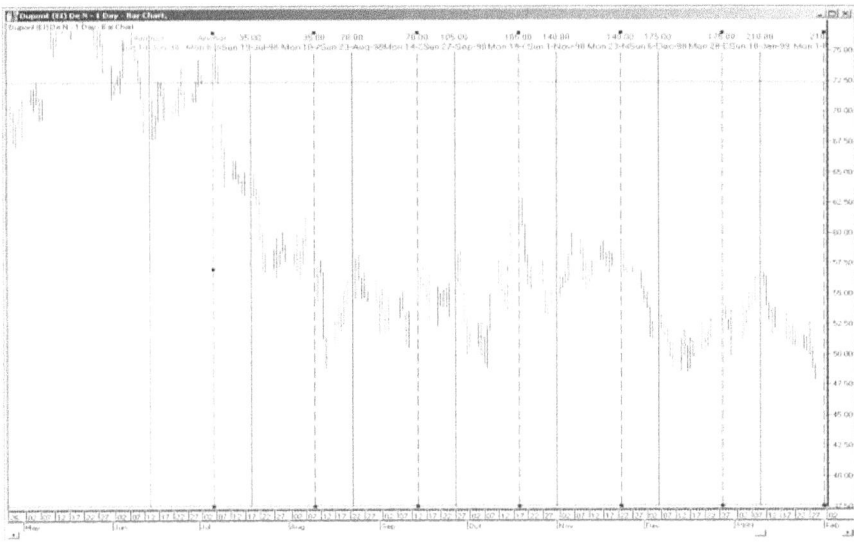

Patterns and Ellipses

50-WEEKLY CYCLE

The following illustrated 50-weekky cycle is very dominant as you can see. See how closely the chart fits this weekly cycle. You should initially check this cycle before you do anything. It's usually accurate to 1 week on each side of the cycle point.

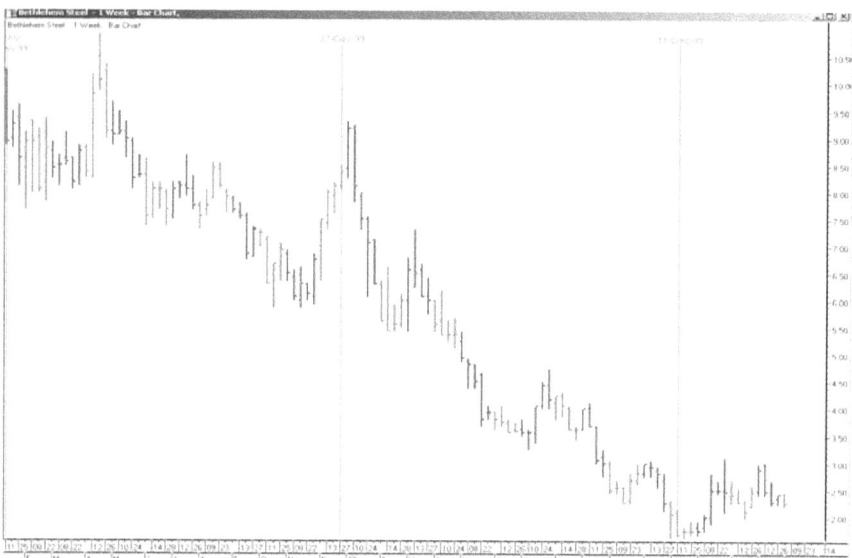

37.5 WEEKLY CYCLE

The 37.5 weekly cycle is 2nd most important. Always check this cycle for timing. Remember that more than one cycle can be working at any one time.

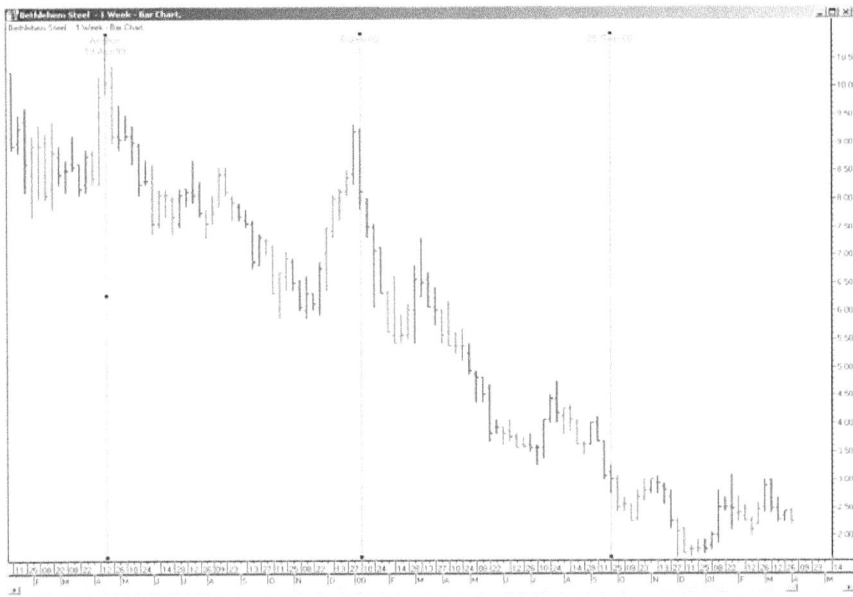

Patterns and Ellipses

25 WEEKLY CYCLE

Now look at the 25 weekly cycle. See how this works with the market. As you can see in this example it works to within the normal bar on each side of the timing point.

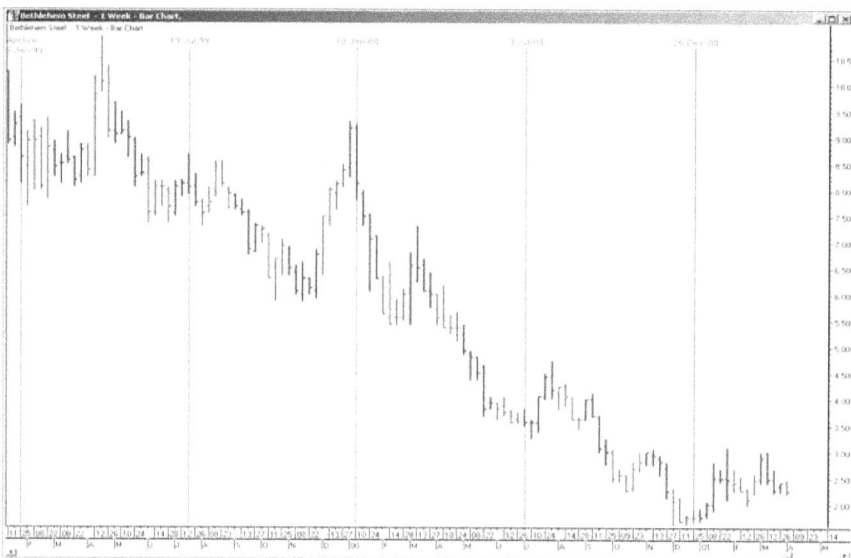

17 WEEKLY CYCLE

The 17 weekly cycle is also important. In this example its accuracy is very respectable. On most points it was within the bar on each side of the timing point accuracy.

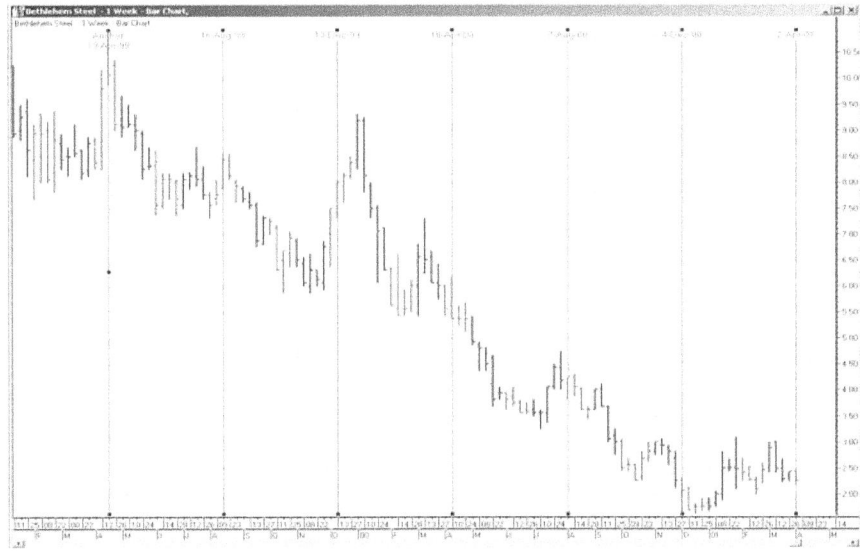

Patterns and Ellipses

12.5 WEEKLY CYCLE

The 12.5 weekly cycle works in this chart example. Most of the timing point hits were very respectable.

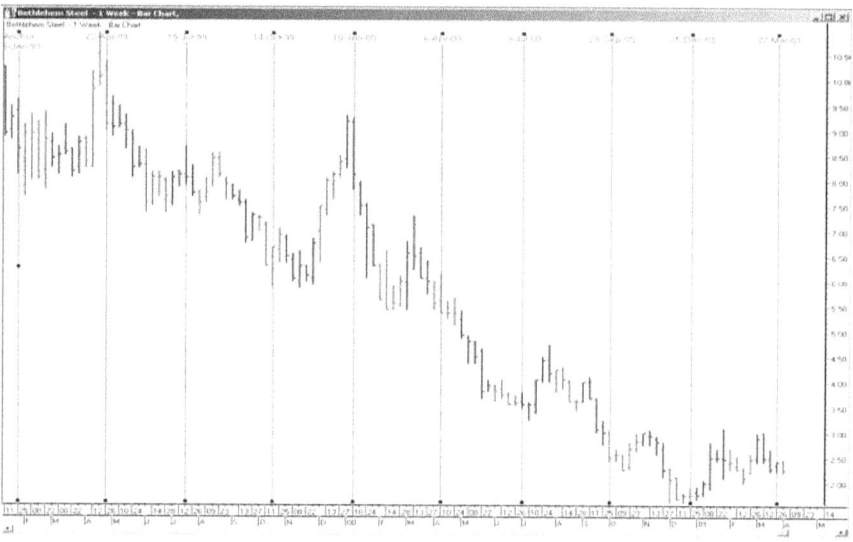

8.5 WEEKLY CYCLE

The 8.5 weekly cycle in this example was fairly close, but not as accurate as some of the previous weekly timing examples.

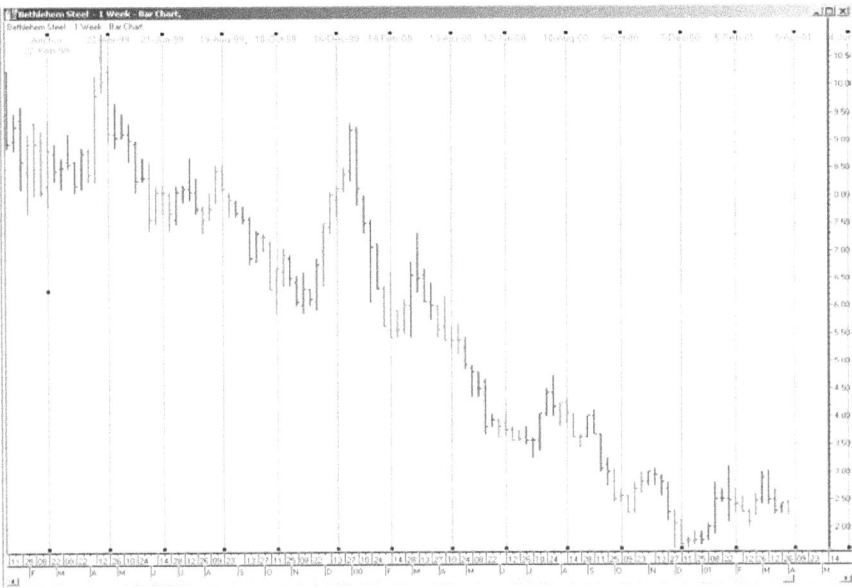

Patterns and Ellipses

6.25 WEEKLY CYCLE

The next chart illustrates the 6.25 weekly cycle. It is one of the more accurate cycles and as you can see it worked nicely on the following chart.

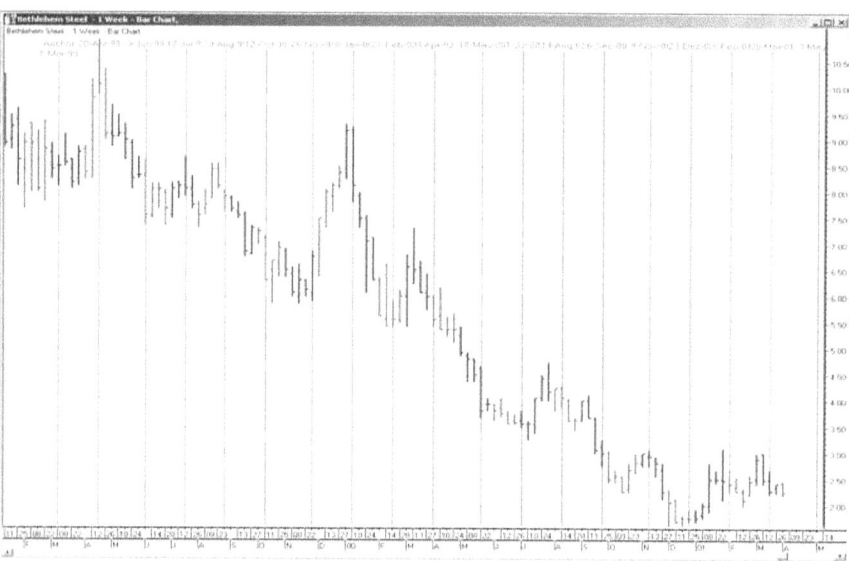

Larry Jacobs

CONVERT WEEKLY CYCLE INTO 21.87 DAYS

In the following example we have converted the 6.25 weekly cycle into the daily cycle. 6.25 x 7 = 43.75 calendar days /2 = 21.87 days

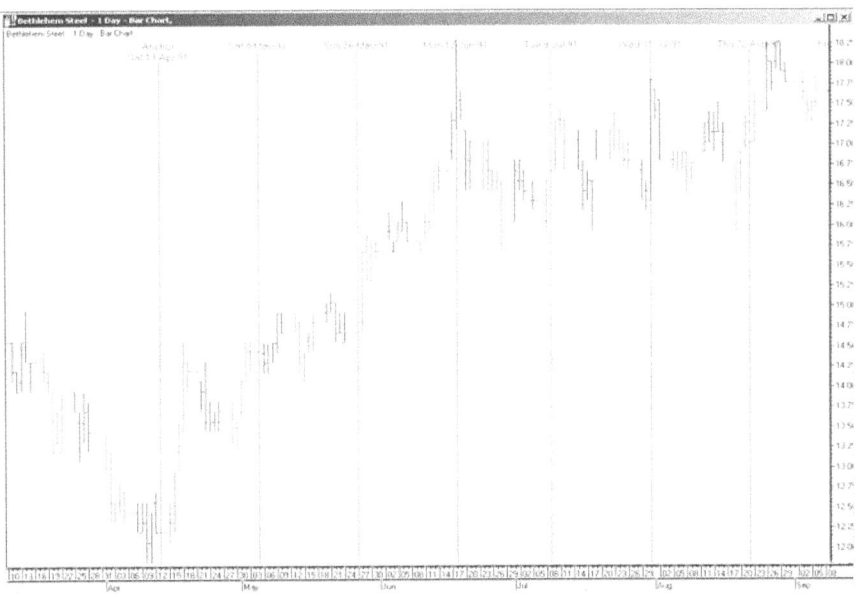

Patterns and Ellipses

CONVERT WEEKLY CYCLE INTO 14.58 DAYS

In this example we have converted the weekly cycle down even further into 14.58 days. 6.25 x 7 = 43.75 calendar days /3 = 14.58 days

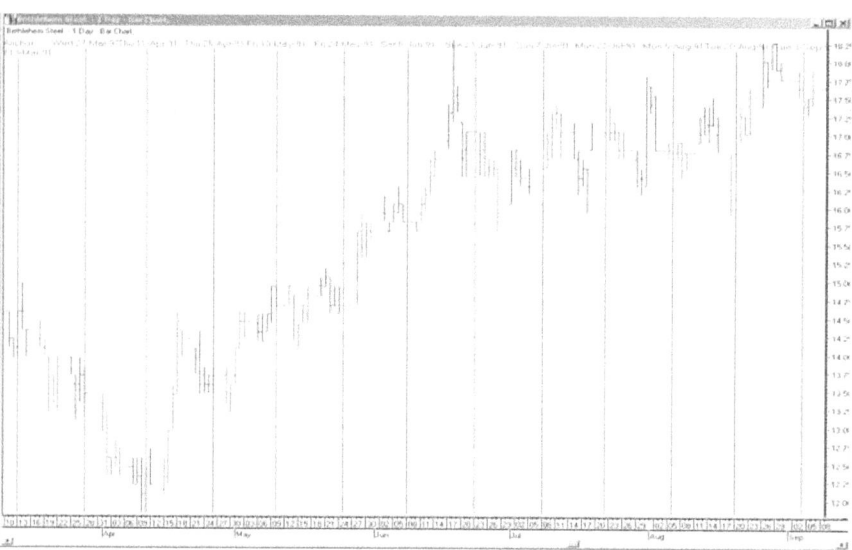

Larry Jacobs

CONVERT WEEKLY CYCLE INTO 10.93 DAYS

In this example we have converted the weekly cycle even further into 10.93 days. 6.25 x 7 = 43.75 calendar days /4 = 10.93 days

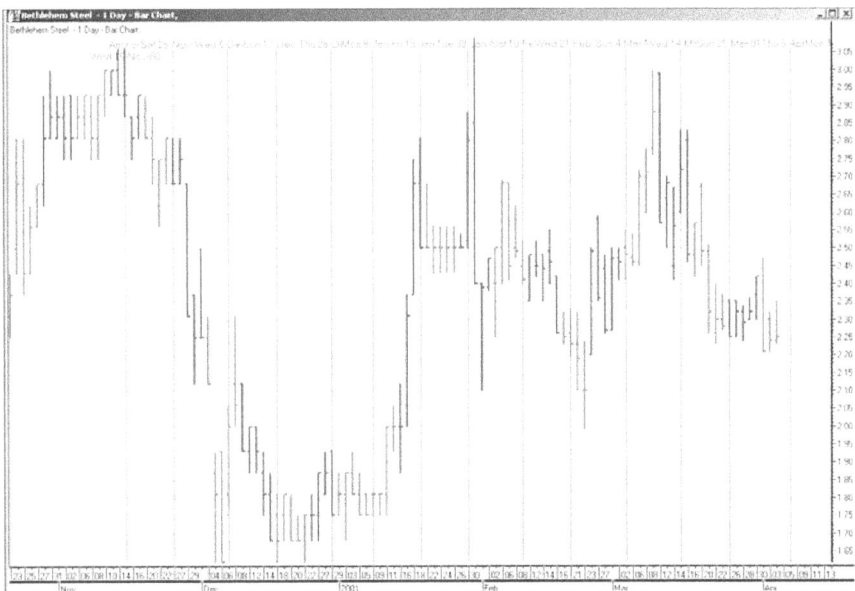

Patterns and Ellipses

CONVERT WEEKLY CYCLE INTO 7.29 DAYS

In the following example we have converted the weekly cycle even further into 7.29 days. 6.25 x 7 = 43.75 calendar days /6 = 7.29 days

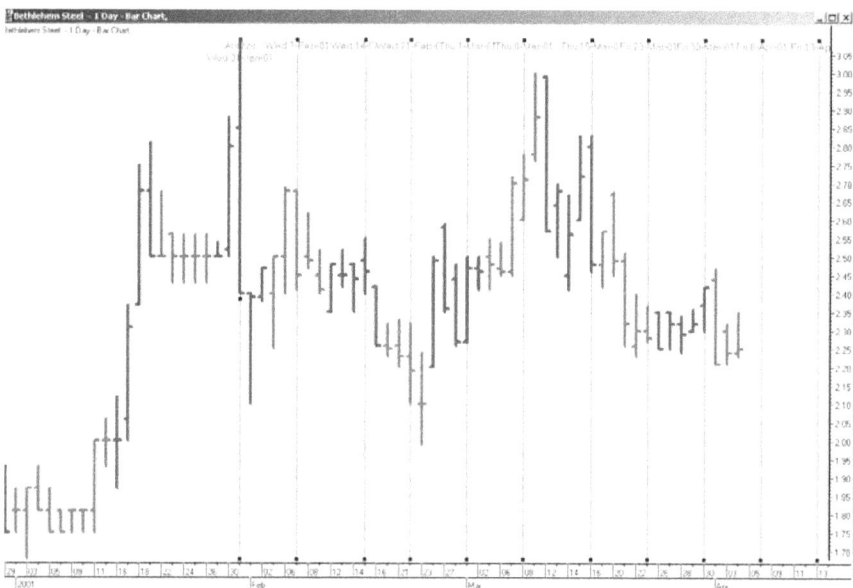

Larry Jacobs

CONVERT WEEKLY CYCLE INTO 3.65 DAYS

In the following example converting the weekly cycle even further into 3.65 days. 6.25 x 7 = 43.75 calendar days /12 = 3.65 days

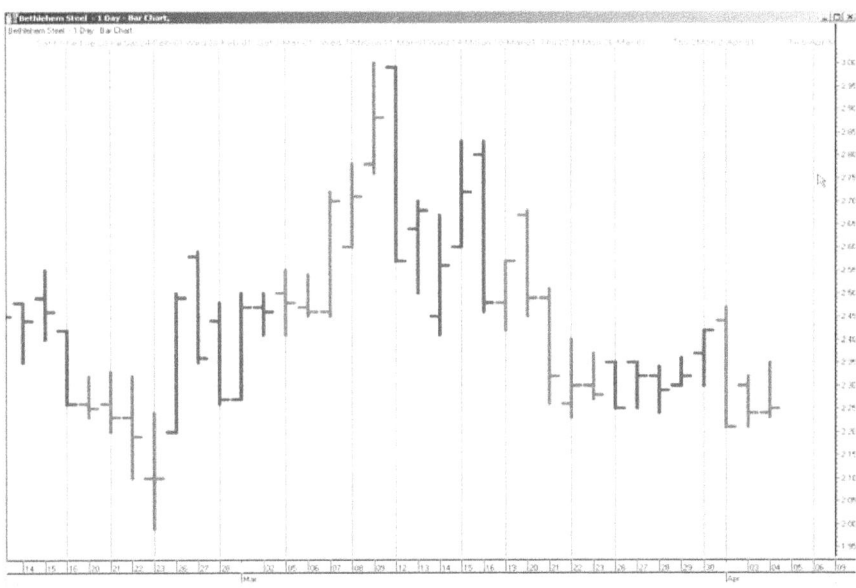

Patterns and Ellipses

ASPECTS

Planetary aspects are very important to watch for changes in trends around the key cycle times of:

50 weeks

25 weeks

17 weeks

12.5 weeks

8.5 weeks

6.25 weeks

21.87 days

14.58 days

11.93 days

7.29 days

3.65 days

Aspects occur between two different plants and with the Sun in the following aspects:

Conjunction 0?

Opposition 180?

Sextile 60?

Square 90?

Trine 120?

Semisextile 30?

Semisquare 145?

Sesquiquandrate 135?

Biquintile 144?

Quincunx 150?

The Opposition, Sextile, Square and Trine are the most important of the above. The Conjunction, Semisextile, Semisquare, Sesquiquandrate, Biquintile and Quincunx are less important.

Patterns and Ellipses

ASPECTS TIED TO CYCLES

The following aspects should be looked at closely especially when they tie into the cycles given above:

Sun Opposition, Sextile, Square, Trine Mars

Sun Opposition, Sextile, Square, Trine Jupiter

Sun Opposition, Sextile, Square, Trine Saturn

Sun Opposition, Sextile, Square, Trine Uranus

Sun Opposition, Sextile, Square, Trine Neptune

Sun Opposition, Sextile, Square, Trine Pluto

Venus Opposition, Sextile, Square, Trine Mars

Venus Opposition, Sextile, Square, Trine Jupiter

Venus Opposition, Sextile, Square, Trine Saturn

Venus Opposition, Sextile, Square, Trine Uranus

Venus Opposition, Sextile, Square, Trine Neptune

Venus Opposition, Sextile, Square, Trine Pluto

Mars Opposition, Sextile, Square, Trine Jupiter

Mars Opposition, Sextile, Square, Trine Saturn

Mars Opposition, Sextile, Square, Trine Uranus

Mars Opposition, Sextile, Square, Trine Neptune

Larry Jacobs

Mars Opposition, Sextile, Square, Trine Pluto

Jupiter Opposition, Sextile, Square, Trine Saturn
Jupiter Opposition, Sextile, Square, Trine Uranus
Jupiter Opposition, Sextile, Square, Trine Neptune
Jupiter Opposition, Sextile, Square, Trine Pluto

Saturn Opposition, Sextile, Square, Trine Uranus
Saturn Opposition, Sextile, Square, Trine Neptune
Saturn Opposition, Sextile, Square, Trine Pluto

Uranus Opposition, Sextile, Square, Trine Neptune
Uranus Opposition, Sextile, Square, Trine Pluto

Neptune Opposition, Sextile, Square, Trine Pluto

The following charts give you some examples of how planetary aspects affect certain markets. Look at them closely.

Patterns and Ellipses

SUN SEXTILE MARS

Notice in this example of December Corn how the Sun Sextile Mars showed intermediate tops and bottoms to the week.

SUN SEXTILE JUPITER

In this example Sun Sextile Jupiter gave a many minor tops and bottoms with December Corn.

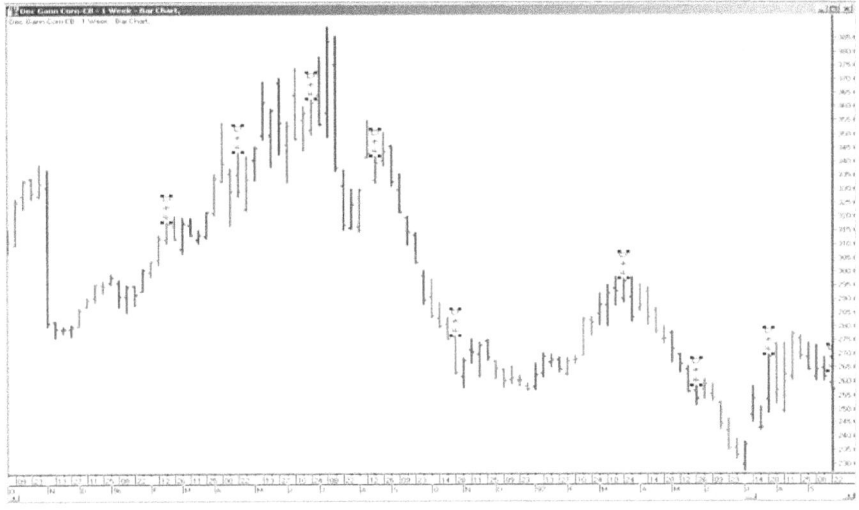

Patterns and Ellipses

SUN SEXTILE SATURN

In this example Sun Sextile Saturn gave a large number of minor tops with December Corn.

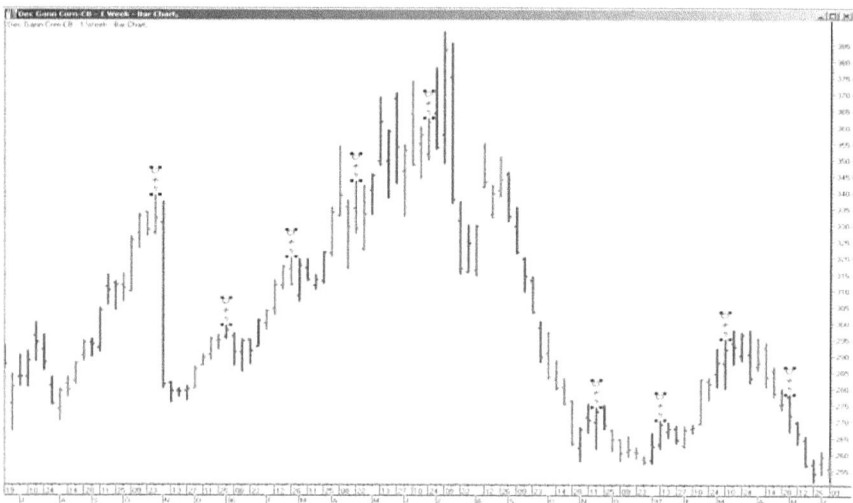

Larry Jacobs

SUN SEXTILE URANUS

In this example with December Gold Sun Sextile Uranus gave many intermediate tops and bottoms.

Patterns and Ellipses

SUN SEXTILE NEPTUNE

In this example of the Australian Dollar see how the Sun Sextile Neptune called many intermediate tops to the week.

Larry Jacobs

SUN SEXTILE PLUTO

In the following example of December British Petroleum Sun Sextile Pluto gave many intermediately highs on the weekly chart.

Patterns and Ellipses

VENUS SEXTILE MARS

In this example of December Copper the Venus Sextile Mars there were several minor highs given throughout the trend by this signal.

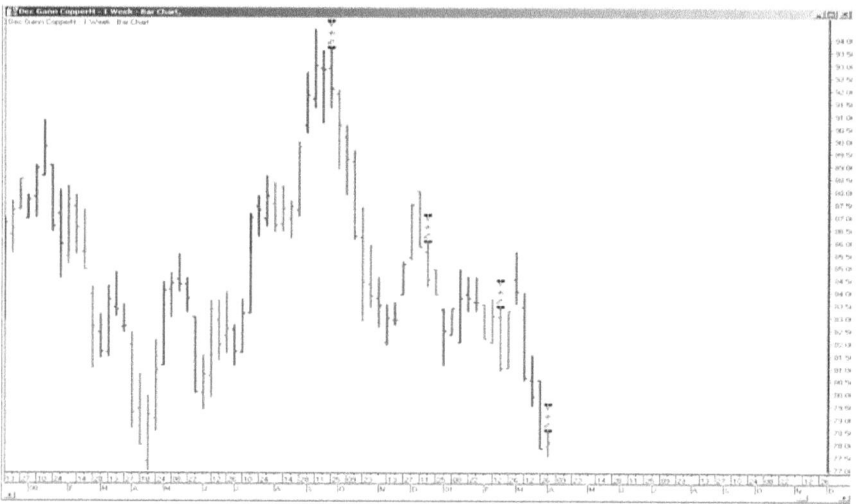

VENUS SEXTILE JUPITER

This example of Venus Sextile Jupiter gave a large number of minor highs in this chart of May Corn.

Patterns and Ellipses

VENUS SEXTILE SATURN

In this example of December Japanese Yen the Venus Sextile Saturn gave a lot of minors highs in its topping formation.

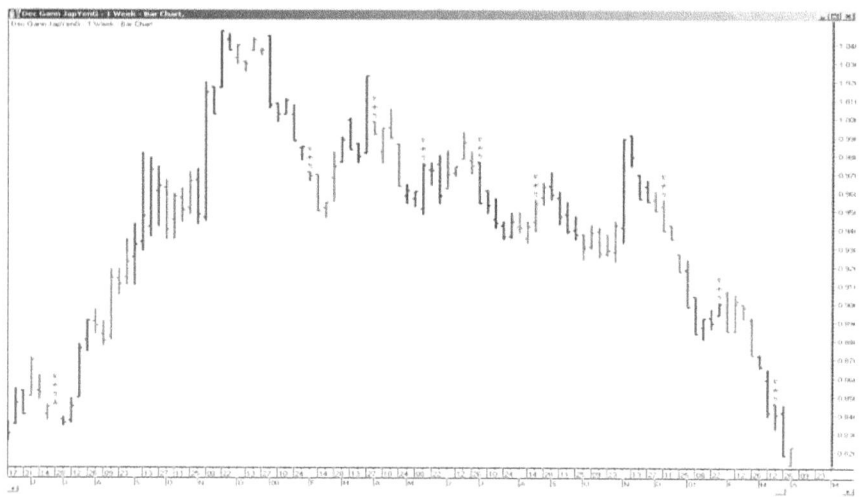

Larry Jacobs

VENUS SEXTILE URANUS

In this example of December Coffee the Venus Sextile Uranus signal gave a large number of minor highs in the downtrend.

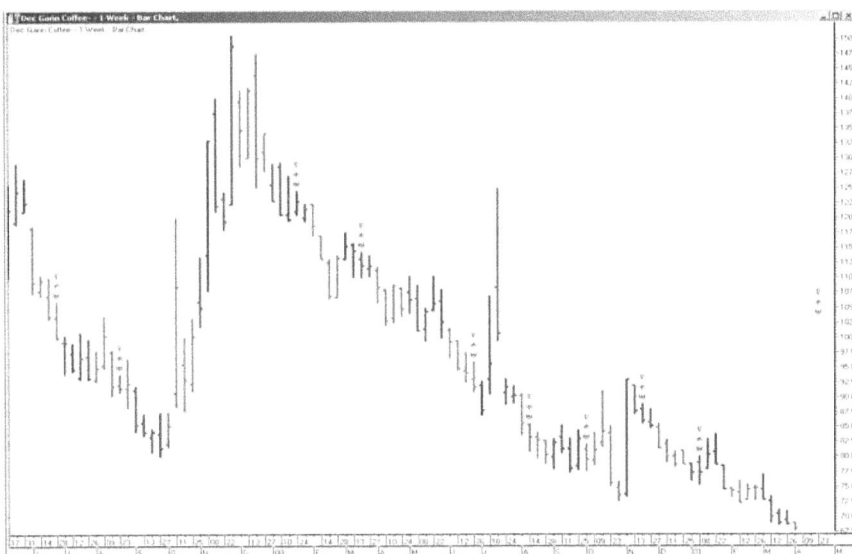

Patterns and Ellipses

VENUS SEXTILE NEPTUNE

In this example of December Cotton the Venus Sextile Neptune gave a large number of intermediate highs in the uptrend within 1 – 2 bars.

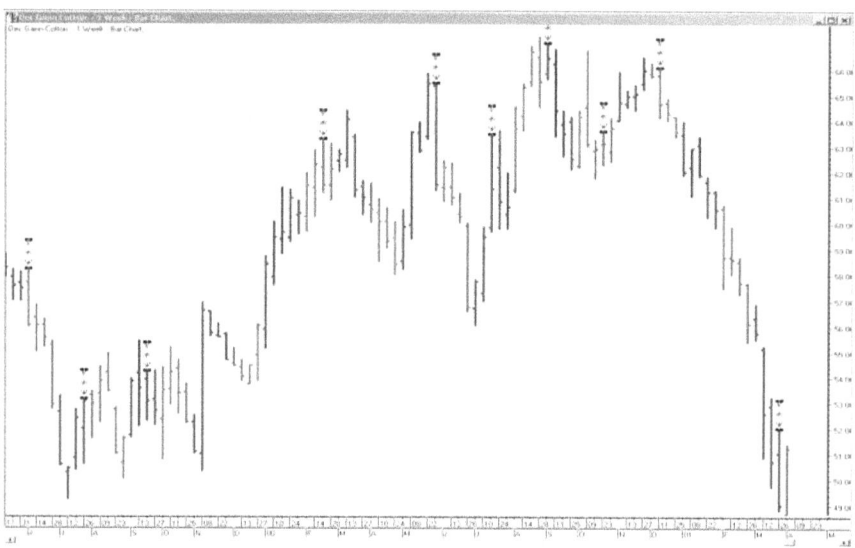

Larry Jacobs

VENUS SEXTILE JUPITER

In this example of May Oats the Venus Sextile Jupiter signal gave minor highs and lows.

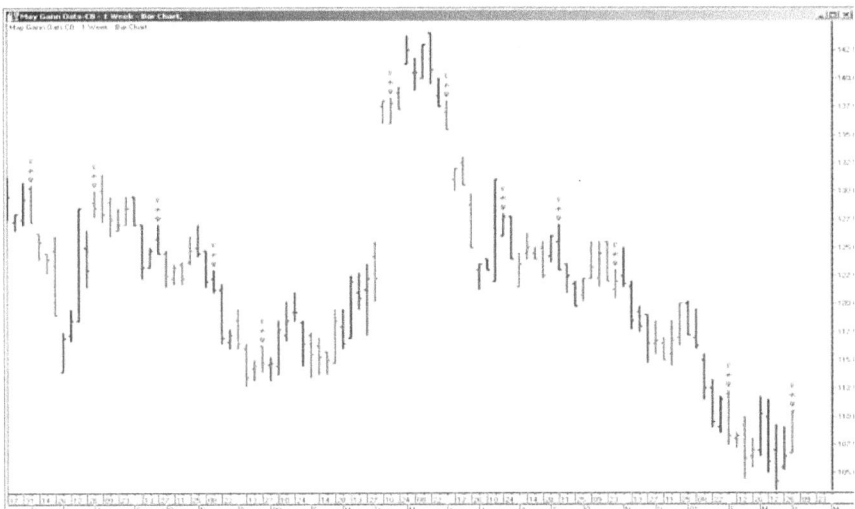

Patterns and Ellipses

ASTROLOGICAL TIMING

In George Bayer's course he felt that you could determine when there was a change in a stock or commodity by the value sign each planet occupies at they move. He said that when the planets cross three values there would be a probable change of trend. The values are:

13 DEGREES 38'12" Taurus

16 DEGREES 21'48" Virgo

15 DEGREEES Capricorn.

The sign symbols are listed in the figure below. Notice the Glyphs on the left side for each of the signs on the right side. Try to remember what these Glyphs look like.

SIGN SYMBOLS

Legend of Symbols used in the Ephemeris:

Planet Symbols		Aspect Symbols		Zodiac Sign Symbols	
☉	Sun	☌	Conjunction 0°	♈	Aries
☽	Moon	☍	Opposition 180°	♉	Taurus
☿	Mercury	✶	Sextile 60°	♊	Gemini
♀	Venus	☐	Square 90°	♋	Cancer
♂	Mars	△	Trine 120°	♌	Leo
♃	Jupiter	Q	Quintile 72°	♍	Virgo
♄	Saturn	⋎	SemiSextile 30°	♎	Libra
♅	Uranus	∠	SemiSquare 45°	♏	Scorpio
♆	Neptune	⚼	Sesquiquadrate 135°	♐	Sagittarius
♇	Pluto	⚻	Quincrunx 150°	♑	Capricorn
☊	True North			♒	Aquarius
⊕	Earth			♓	Pisces

Patterns and Ellipses

VISUAL EPHEMERIS

We are using a visual Ephemeris, which gives basically planetary places. It contains the position of all planets on a daily basis. We are only interested in the planet's motion in longitude. Declination or latitude is not considered. When the planets pass through the three special values give above there is usually a change of trend in the market place.

In the following three instances we look at a Dupont chart taken randomly from the stocks we are looking at. Dupont made a top on 3/14/1997 when Jupiter crosses through 15? Capricorn. See the following figure.

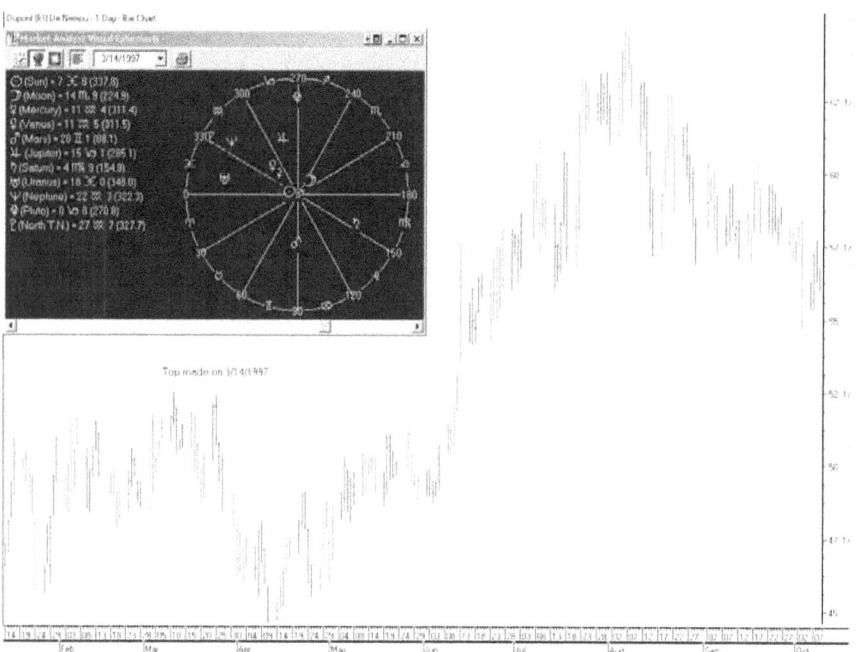

In the next chart you see Dupont turns up on 5/3/1997 after Venus crosses through 13 Degrees 38'12" Taurus. See the following chart.

98

Larry Jacobs

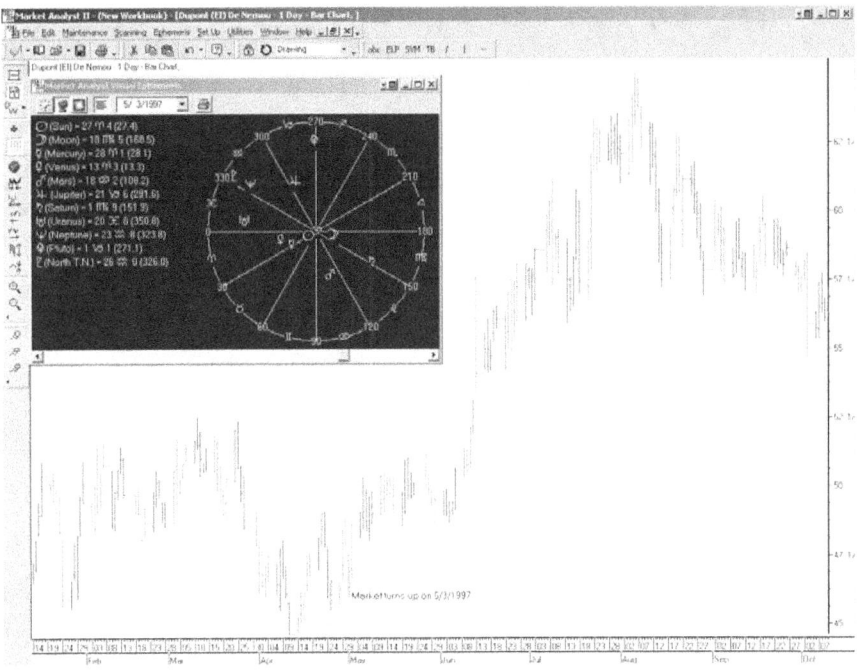

Next you see a major top on 6/6/1997 when Jupiter crossed through 15? Capricorn. Also notice on the visual Ephemeris that Mars and Saturn are also getting ready to cross through 16 Degrees 21'48" Virgo within just a few days. That's three signals occurring nearly at once making this a major top. See the following chart.

These signals don't tell us the direction of the next move. One should use other methods to determine the direction. All we know is that a change in trend is due on a certain day. Certain planets have different effects on stocks and commodities. From trial and error it is easy to see which planets are affecting each individual stock or commodity. The moon also has an effect. It travels much faster, so it will therefore give many more signals. Most of these are short term in nature.

Patterns and Ellipses

Larry Jacobs

ASTROLOGICAL CRITICAL DEGREES

Each stock or commodity reacts at particular degrees and minute of the Zodiac to one or two planets in one or two positions. In the following example of December Corn, you will find that it reacts almost exactly and changes trend when Mars crosses 2? 0' of a sign. Every major turn of the commodity hit that particular degree in this chart and turned trend to the very day!

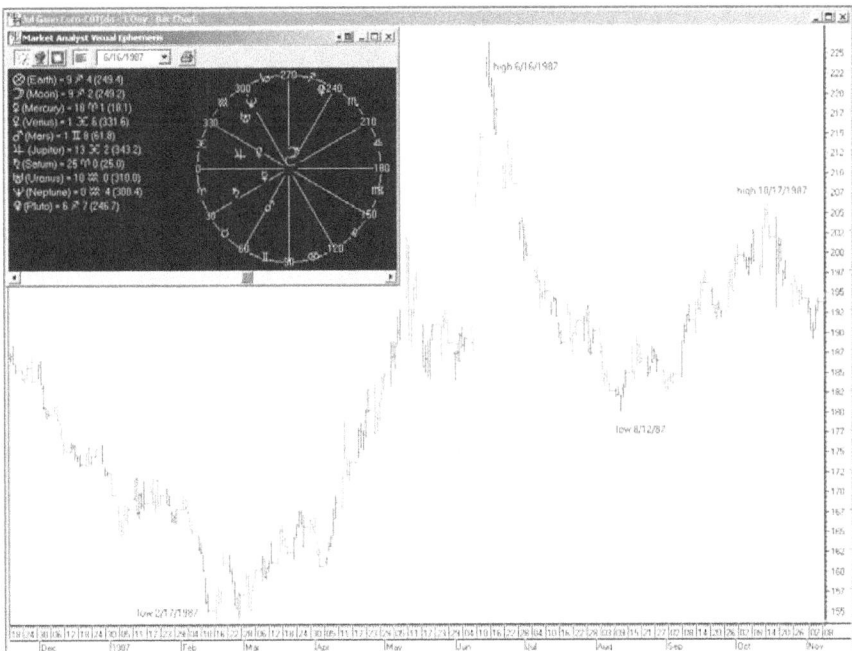

Patterns and Ellipses

Larry Jacobs

GANN PLANETARY LINES

The Gann Planetary Lines are based upon the position of the planets in relation to the earth, sun or sidereal. Gann did a great deal of analysis where he used the longitude of planets as price support and resistance. Some early Gann charts show how Gann drew by hand the angles of the planets on his charts. Gann's theory was that certain planets affected certain markets. The translation of planet longitude to price is achieved by, for example, establishing that 270 degrees will be drawn on a chart at 27 cents or $2.70 or $27 or $270, whichever is in the range of the data. To allow for prices outside the 0 to 360 degree range, the price has 360 degrees added to it, for example after 27 cents the next price would be 63 cents. Harmonics should also be displayed with these lines. For instance, the angle on a particular day may be 270 degrees (as described above), but if four harmonics are displayed, price lines are seen at 27 cents, 36 cents, 45 cents, 54 cents, and then the repeated baseline and 63 cents and so on. Baselines should be bold while harmonics are lighter so that it is easy to distinguish between the two types of lines. See the following chart of Caterpillar Tractor with planetary lines drawn divided into 4 divisions between main lines. Lines can be drawn in any division between main lines.

Patterns and Ellipses

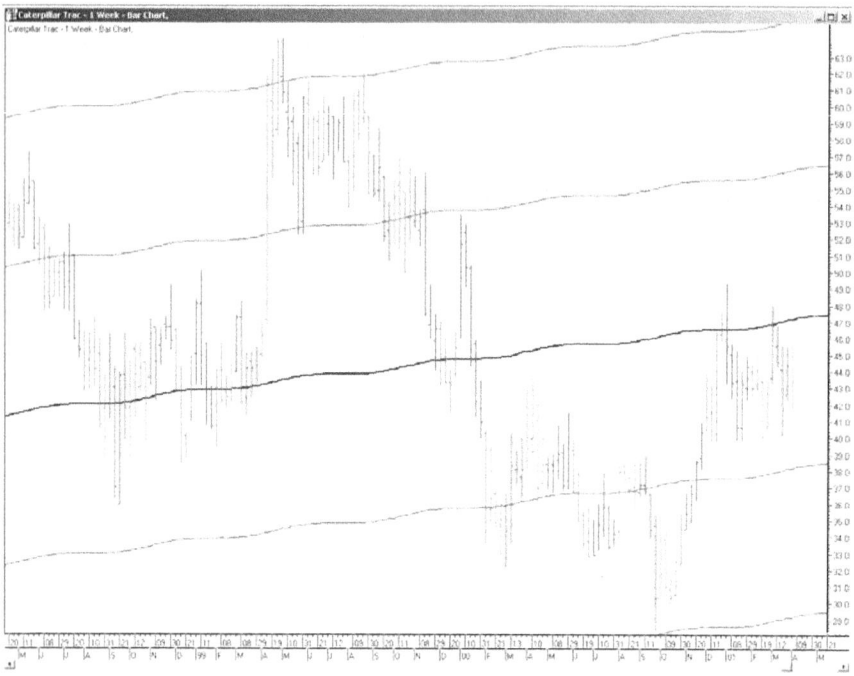

Larry Jacobs

SQUARE OF NINE

Gann used the SQ9 table to determine price targets. The lines created using the SQ9 often reveal support and resistance in the market. When a price is selected on the SQ9 chart, prices at 360 degrees and other selected angles in between are identified and displayed at calculated price levels. Using the SQ9 to display a line at 45 degrees, the price is calculated 45 degrees from the starting price. In the following example the Square of Nine was drawn on bottoms in the uptrend. The market encountered resistance between the 225 and 270 levels.

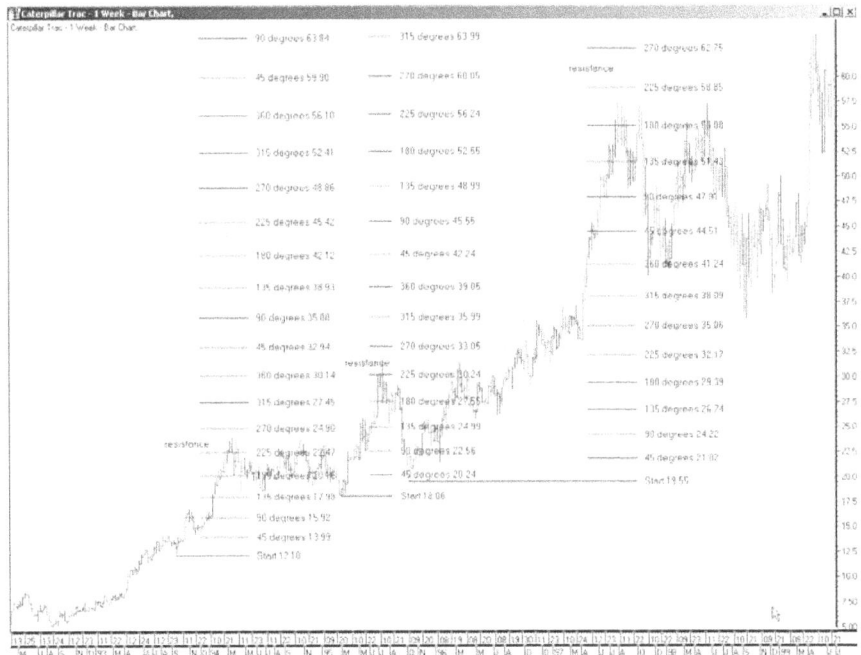

Patterns and Ellipses

STATIC SQUARE OF NINE

The Static Square of Nine (SQ9-S) is used in determining price targets. The lines created using the SQ9-S can reveal support and resistance in the market. This tool differs from the standard Square of Nine in that a starting price does not need to be selected. The starting price (factor) defaults to a value of 1. From this point the selected angles, e.g. 90 degrees, 180 degrees, 270 degrees, 360 degrees, are drawn on a chart as a series of horizontal lines. These lines are drawn indefinitely on the price scale as per the selected angles. Because some commodities trade at values below 1, or trade in values of many thousands (e.g. Dow), a multiplying factor can be applied to the SQ9-S to produce values, which are relevant to the analyzed security. See how support and resistance hit's on the weekly Caterpillar Tractor stock.

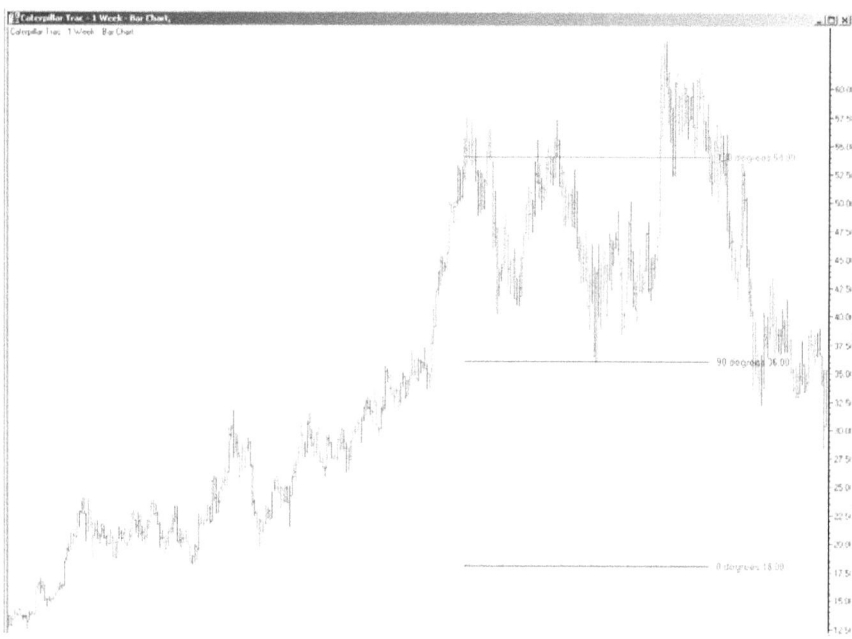

Larry Jacobs

Patterns and Ellipses

PYRAPOINT

Pyrapoint is an excellent Square of Nine and channeling technique discovered by Don E. Hall. Here is a story reproduced by permission of Traders World Magazine. Don Hall is the author.

Probably no one in the trading world has received more discussion than W.D. Gann. Discussions of the famous trader have ranged from awe and admiration to downright disbelief. Some of us found this to be one of the foundation bricks of reason for studying his sometimes- complex trading life.

Having been in the markets in both cash and futures since the mid 1950's, it became evident to me that not all of the information, which I found to be touted even in those early days was 100%. This is no surprise to most of you as readers of a technical source such as Traders World magazine. More than a surprise, I found it to be a challenge.

The percentage of correct trades attributable to Mr. Gann just did not fit the pattern, which was my lot in my own hedging and trading. Thus I set my goal to first find out as much as I could as to the validity of the claims. My acquaintance and friendship with Mr. "Reno" Alghini, a friend and close trading associate of Mr. Gann, started me in earnest to the next goal. It also gave me the road map of my next challenge.

"Reno" often commented that when Gann went to the pit, he always carried the Pythagorean Cube (Square of Nine as we know it), and many times, nothing else for support. This fact made me realize that I had my work assignment.

Gann's record in public and under scrutiny made one conclusion evident to me: it just had to be simpler than that to which I had been exposed in books, seminars, and courses – just had to be!

From this point in my studies, roughly halfway through the 45 years which I have determined this market interest, I began Gann studies in nearly 100% of my efforts. The reason: no one to whom

I had knowledge had done so well in trading, nor nearly so consistently. If one needs a guide to hang his or her goals upon, in my opinion, it is CONSISTENCY. Even with his high percentage of accuracy, we are shown that Gann still maintained a very good ratio of dollars earned per trade – and he apparently did so with a minimum of risk. This meant one thing to me: he had to know what he was trading, when to trade it, when to be dormant to a trade, and at what point to be in and/or get out. It seems to me that these are worthy goals with which to trade by any standards.

Thus our quest for more and more information on the Pythagorean Cube seemed to be justified. After all, if it were the tool that it seemed to be when Gann was under fire by the press as well as in the pit, why then should it not be worthy of our 100% effort? It was and is. Thus the birth of PYRAPOINT: A Trade Analogy.

Just what is this system called PYRAPOINT: A Trade Analogy? In the simplest of terms, it is the unraveling of the Pythagorean Cube.

As we have stated in an earlier article, we likely aren't the first to see the almost mystic market waves and, indeed, the full moves as they relate to the Pythagorean Cube. PYRAPOINT: A Trade Analogy, simply gives us a plan to use these wonderful moves, and a place to get (or stay) out of a loss or losses.

The important word in the prior paragraph is "SIMPLY." No system or plan is of much use to us, in our opinion, if it involves so much effort and research per trade that we cannot ACT on the recommendation. The market moves much too quickly for very involved criteria. It is our belief that Gann did not have that much time either, as determined by the number trades credited to his per-hour of trading.

We are convinced that one needs a system that provides early and continuing indications of market action. We believe that one needs a road map approach. We are also convinced that this recognizable direction must be familiar enough to us for our action without hesitation. Confidence – right?

Patterns and Ellipses

Herein lies the true basis for discipline, that all-important factor for successful trading. We need to see the opportunity, read it for target and for time – then act. Call it confidence – call it discipline – it is the answer to successful trades – simply and quickly. We don't even necessarily require a computer if we have the chart of question and recognize the "stop and go lights."

The plot thickens as to reasons for unraveling the Pythagorean Cube.

We are happy to report that our serious students have found our teachings in PYRAPOINT: A Trade Analogy, to yield to them a better trading life. Some have graciously given us a "best" rating. The single-most heard praise is that it simply makes sense – that it yields a reason for our position of entry and exit – that it gives a track to follow for full fruition of a trade – and that (if we follow the six simple rules) we simply do have a better bottom line. We believe that this is what it is all about!

This doesn't mean that our grade card does not indicate that we haven't experienced the "normal 3%" who aren't claiming to be in this group. We not only understand this, we anticipate some reluctance to read or study 300 pages (especially with so much information "out there" today). Our comment however is to recall that nearly half of the pages are pictures (charts). We expect to confirm all of our text. Because we have elected to give you book owners the time advantage while waiting for the professional publishing house, we have been asked to send to you the full-color prototype of the book from our office until the publisher can get "on line." We have done this. In this process, we ink-jet print each page individually, place them in our covers and have them professionally bound with binders which allow you to lay the book open to study, compare charts, or make notes at your discretion. This is a workbook of knowledge for your better trading. It is to show you what is actually going on in this world of trading via the Pythagorean Cube. It is not to place on the mantel as décor. Actually our students relate that it is revealing to other fields as well – but certainly the markets.

Although we have honestly had no direct negative critique, we understand that we have been discussed in a chat room environment wherein a person felt that we had been a bit careless since he had found a page upside down. Some of the charts are at 90 degrees to the pages of text to show a point, but I personally must take that debit, and I do apologize – it gets a bit late at the office on some editions for us old fellers! I also apologize that the prototype requires flipping a page of text to fit a chart occasionally. I have faith in all of you to overcome – so long as you are getting the information to assist your life – AND THIS WILL! One last critique was that it seemed a lot of information to learn the "Square of Nine." I hear you. I tried it for 20 years. Friend, if you have learned the art and calculations of the mystic diagonals, where to place your entries and exits, where to expect changes (which direction and how much), how to regulate your squares for calculation, and then have developed good rules to control your marketing and your discipline – then I agree with you. I just haven't met a person who could show me these things. I am certain that this or these person(s) exist – otherwise I would undoubtedly not have found it to share. One last item for this topic: we have offered to answer your questions relative to our interpretations to assist you for a period of six months. So talk to us in the chat room per Traders World magazine as invited. We care, and we want to answer your concerns should they not be on the web FAQ.

As stated in the book, PYRAPOINT: A Trade Analogy, we have other reasons why we feel that it is truly "the answer" for most of us. The Pythagorean Cube and Theories are of much earlier origins than Pythagoras' discoveries brought back to Greece from his trek to Egypt. In fact, they are evident in the Great Pyramid and other architecture dating back to 2500 B.C. And as stated the book, it does make one wonder what really took place in that 2000 plus years era, since Pythagoras brought it to the Greeks in the first millennium A.D. It is from here that we began our education in the "modern sense" by the teachings of Pythagoras, sometimes

Patterns and Ellipses

referred to as the "father of modern mathematics" – especially trigonometry, algebraic equations of floating decimals, etc.

At this point let us emphasize that Gann was a particularly good mathematician. This was another clue to our further quest for answers as to how he was so accomplished. His research was quite extensive, even to countries besides Egypt, but he had this all behind him when under fire in the pit, and apparently relied heavily on the notorious Pythagorean Cube. It had to be basic – and it is. It had to be simple – and it is. It had to be accurate for both price and time – and it is. Above all, it had to be far more accessible and more rapidly understood than most of the complicated endeavors to which he is credited. Think about it! How much of what you see attributed to his success in the trading pit could he have done without multiple tools of assistance?

Personally, I have no problem with any of the interpretations of the many varieties of methodologies concerning W.D. Gann. My hat is off to many scholars as they have unwound fact after fact from his work. My point in this discussion is that there are dozens of productions of theories on his methodology, ranging from math to astrology, with many combinations – and with merit for the most part.

The problem that I do have in my years of study is two-fold: (1) to assimilate a profitable trading plan from all of my books and papers which I have collected for two or three decades, as they relate to Gann's works and teachings, and (2) to sort all of the mass of information into a simple and usable plan for trading.

Again, I believe that Gann did his analogy for a trade quickly and accurately with tools, which were available to him at the moment of truth – the moment to ACT on a given trade.

Again, it just had to be simpler than most Gann presentations of the day.

In our opinion, the answer is Universality, ease of understanding and of interpretation, speed of determination and action, accuracy in all of these factors – the answer is SIMPLICITY. The answer is the unraveling of the Pythagorean Cube in a manner that will allow us PEACE OF MIND AND PROFIT, while not overfeeding our margin account. Mr. Gann was right: the answer is to KNOW your trade. In our opinion, this means to KNOW IT ON THE PYTHAGOREAN CUBE. Believe us – like the carpenter's square, there is a world of education on this 4500-year-old Pythagorean Cube. We must learn to use it to prosper! As the readers of PYRAPOINT: A Trade Analogy have stated, "we must stay on the diagonal highways that the Pythagorean Cube undeniably provides – calculate the squares (the posts) and the fence is there for us" – SIMPLY!

Below see the chart using the Pyrapoint system of trading. Notice how it draws the correct Square of Nine objectives automatically. It also draws the parallel channels.

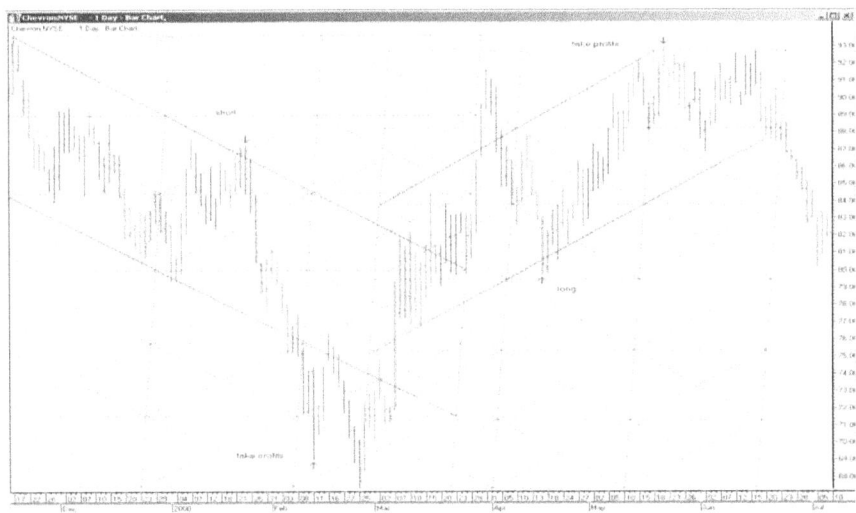

Patterns and Ellipses

CONCENTRIC CIRCLES - TIME

Concentric Circles (CC) are used to draw circles that are probable values of support and resistance in both time and price. The circles are a percentage of a user-defined circle. You have complete control over what percentage values are used in the CC tool and the colors of each of the CC Lines. Common CC values are 50%, 200% and 300%. These values are used as the default values in Market Analyst. CC's are calculated by specifying a starting point in the market, and then moving the cursor to the right until the base circle is the desired size. The other circles are then calculated as a percentage of the original circle. The CC is also enhanced by the ability to specify calendar days, or solar degrees. If calendar days are to be used, Market Analyst calculates the circle based on the number of calendar days between the start and end points resulting in elliptical representation. The following example is taken from the high to the first big low. The expanding circles give you the next two major highs.

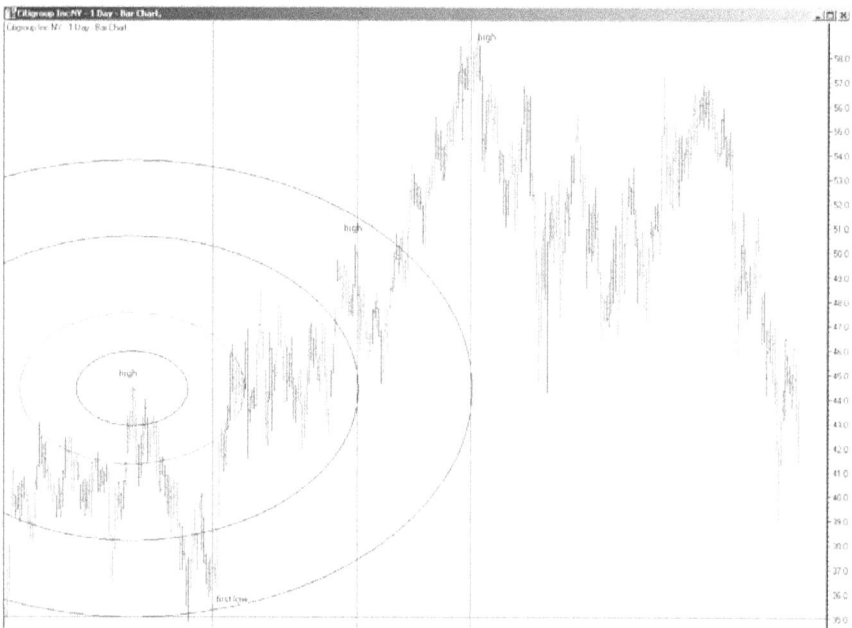

Larry Jacobs

Patterns and Ellipses

CONCENTRIC CIRCLES – PRICE

In this example we use the same chart but set the concentric chart at the low in price rather than time. We then project the concentric circle to expand and give us resistance price levels. Concentric circles are set a ratio to the first. In this case we set it at 50, 200, 300, 450, 700.

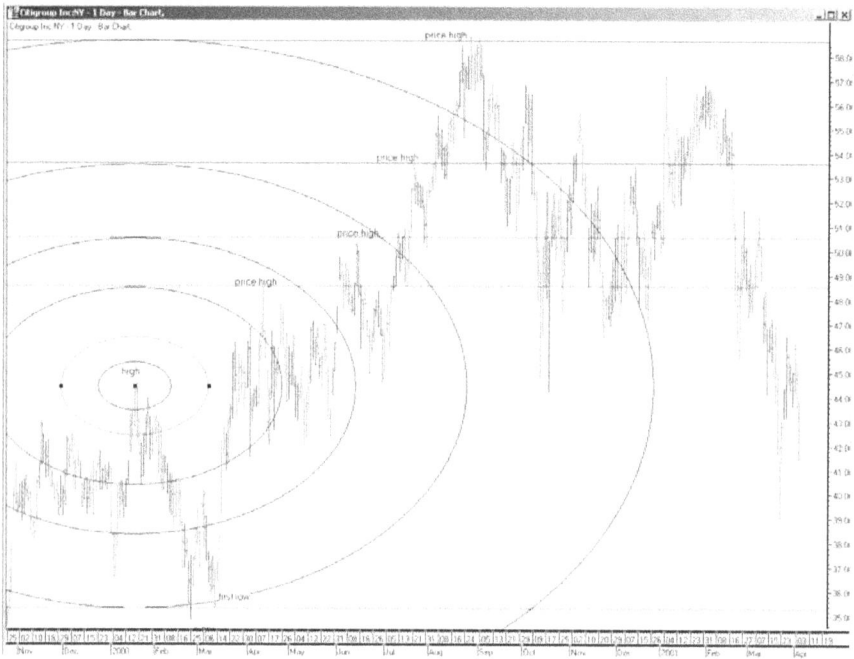

Larry Jacobs

FIBONACCI ARCS

Fibonacci Arcs (FA) are used to draw circular arcs that are probable values of support and resistance based on a market range. Common values are the Fibonacci sequence 38.2%, 50% & 61.8%. If the range went from a low to a high, then the line between the two points is divided up into the percentage ratios. An arc, with its center at the second point, is then drawn through each of the ratios on the line. In this example the entrancement goes all the way to the 50% arc.

Patterns and Ellipses

FIBONACCI FAN

Fibonacci Fans (FF) are used to draw a fan of angled lines that are probable values of support and resistance based on a market range. Common values are the Fibonacci sequence 38.2%, 50% & 61.8%. FF's are calculated by selecting a range in the market. If the range went from a low to a high, then an imaginary line is drawn from the second point vertically down to the price level of the start point. This line is then divided up into the percentage ratios. A fan line is then drawn from the start point through each of the ratios on the imaginary vertical line.

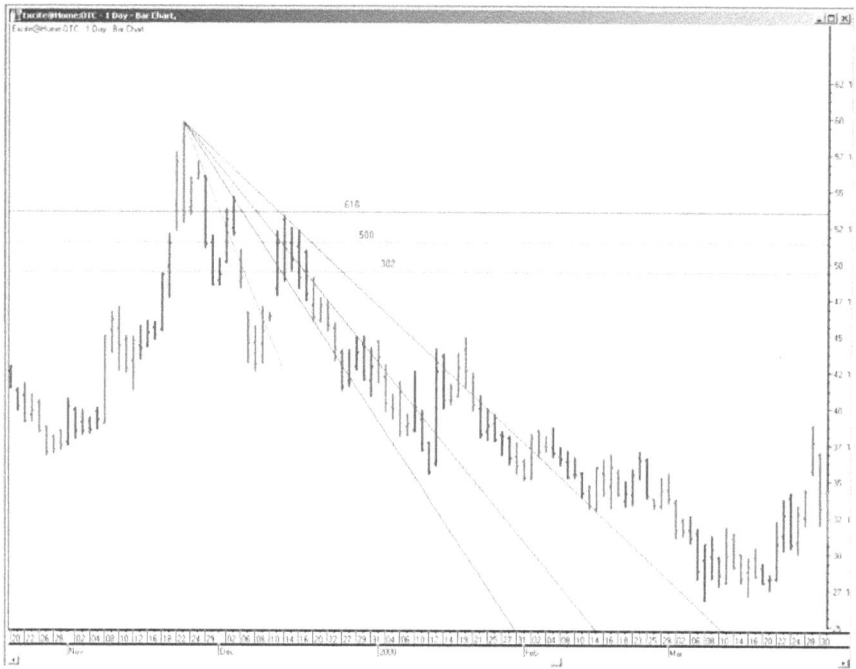

Larry Jacobs

PRICE EXTENSIONS

Price Extensions (PE) are used to specify horizontal lines at price levels which are determined to be probable values of support and resistance based on the markets previous range, and a third extension point. Common values are the Fibonacci sequence 38.2%, 50% & 61.8%. These are used as the default values in Market Analyst. PE's are a percentage of a specified range calculated from a third point. For example, if a market bottom of 2400 was selected as the starting point, and the tool was extended up to a value of 2500 as the market top, then the extension point was selected at the next market bottom of 2450, a PE value of 25% would be 2475. (2450 + 25).

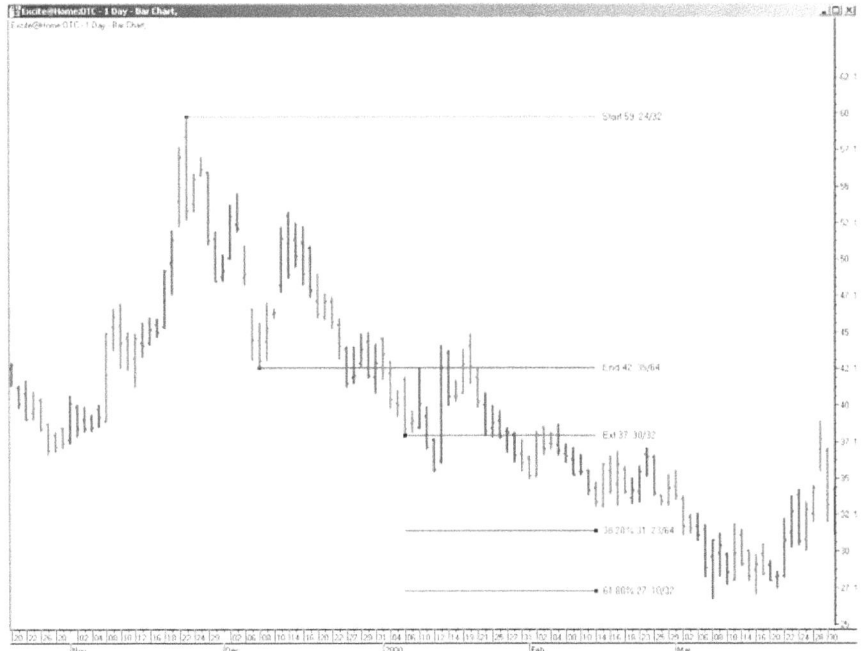

Patterns and Ellipses

PRICE RETRACEMENTS

Price Retracements (PR) are used to specify horizontal lines at price levels which are determined to be probable values of support and resistance based on the market's previous range. Common values are the Fibonacci sequence 38.2%, 50% & 61.8%. PR's are a percentage of a specified range calculated back from the end point. For example, if a market bottom of 2400 was selected as the starting point, and the tool was extended up to a value of 2500 as the market top, then a PR value of 25% would be 2475.

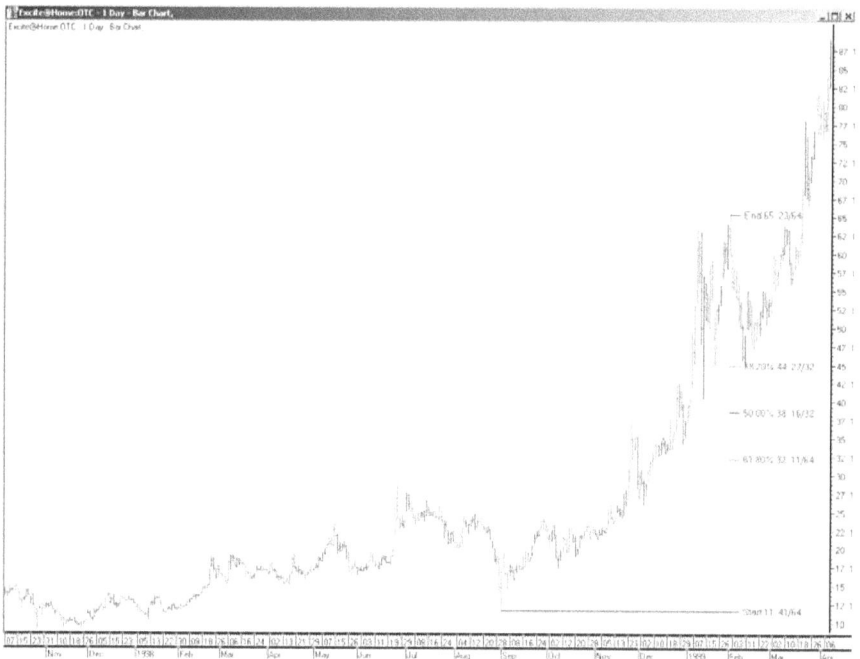

Larry Jacobs

TIME EXTENSIONS

Time Extensions (TE) are used to specify vertical lines at date/time levels which are determined to be probable values of changes in trend based on the market's previous date/time range and a third extension point. Common values are the Fibonacci sequence 138.2%, 150% and 161.8%. TE's are a percentage of a specified date/time range calculated from a third point. For example, if a market bottom at a given date was selected as the starting point, and the tool was extended to a date 100 bars later, then the extension point was selected at the next market change 50 bars further, a TE value of 25% would be 175 bars from the starting date/time.

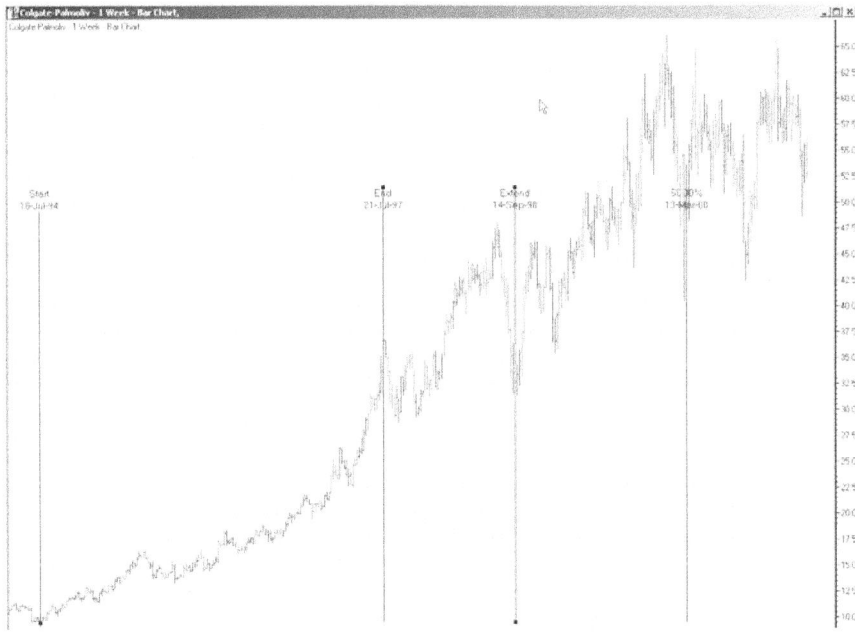

Patterns and Ellipses

Larry Jacobs

TIME RETRACEMENTS

Time Retracements (TR) are used to specify vertical lines at date/time levels which are retracements. Common values are the Fibonacci sequence 138.2%, 150% and 161.8%. TE's are a percentage of a specified date/time range calculated from a third point.

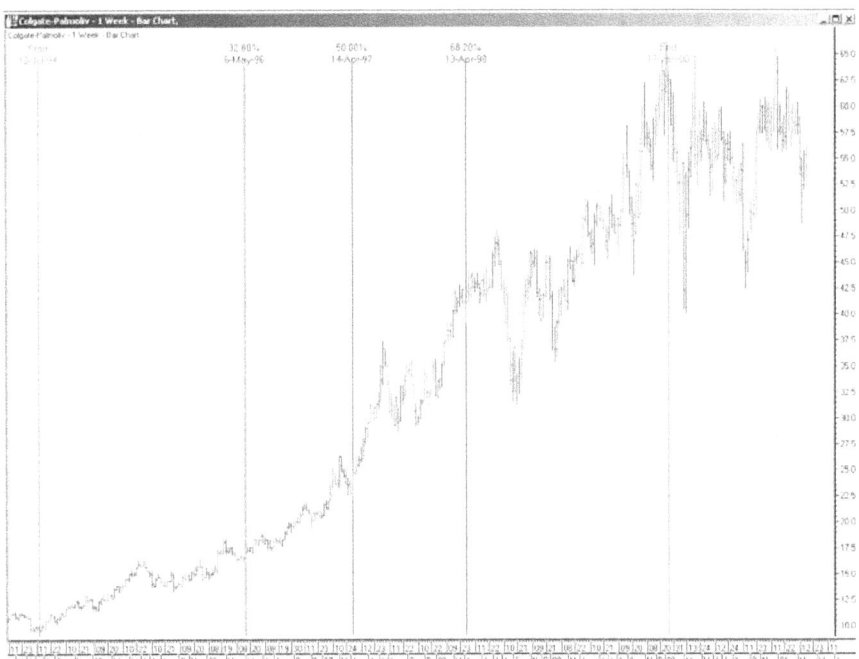

Patterns and Ellipses

ANDREW'S PITCHFORK

Andrew's Pitchfork (AP) is used to form support and resistance lines, which are used to draw channels on a bar chart. AP's are calculated by selecting a starting point and a range (two further points). The central line is drawn from the starting point (A) through the midpoint of the range (B to C). Extra lines are then drawn with the same gradient as the central line from points B & C.

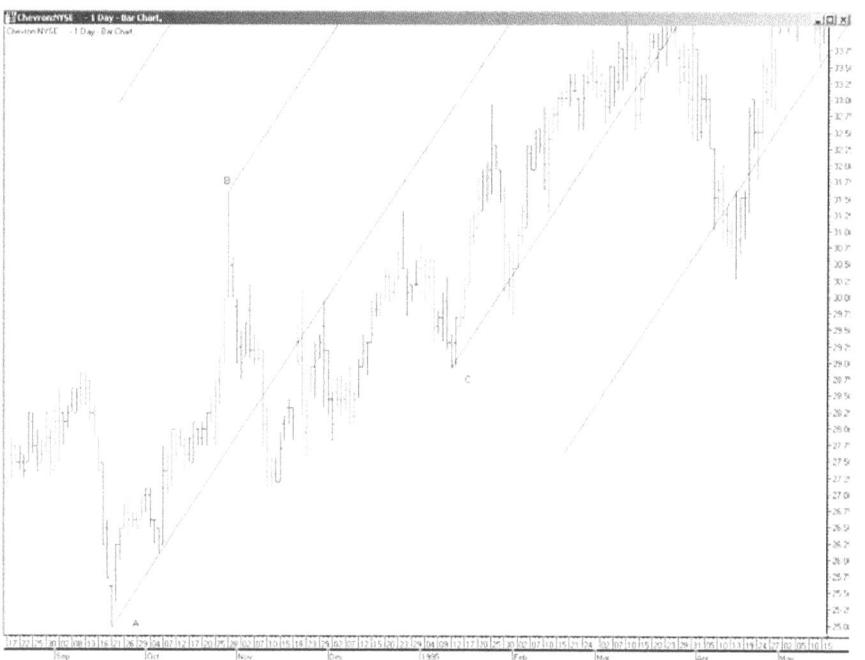

Larry Jacobs

ADX INDICATOR

To calculate the directional movement in a trend (up or down) a range is determined by comparing today's high and low with yesterdays close. If the largest part of today's range is above yesterday's range, the directional movement is plus. If the largest part of today's range is below yesterday's range, the directional movement is minus. If today's range is within yesterday's range, then directional movement is zero. The ADX is calculated as the average of the directional indicators (DIs). To calculate the directional movement in a trend (up or down) a range is determined by comparing today's high and low with yesterdays close. If the largest part of today's range is above yesterday's range, the directional movement is plus. If the largest part of today's range is below yesterday's range, the directional movement is minus. If today's range is within yesterday's range, then directional movement is zero. The ADX is calculated as the average of the directional indicators (DIs). When the red crosses above the green and blue buy and take profits on the top of the run up.

Patterns and Ellipses

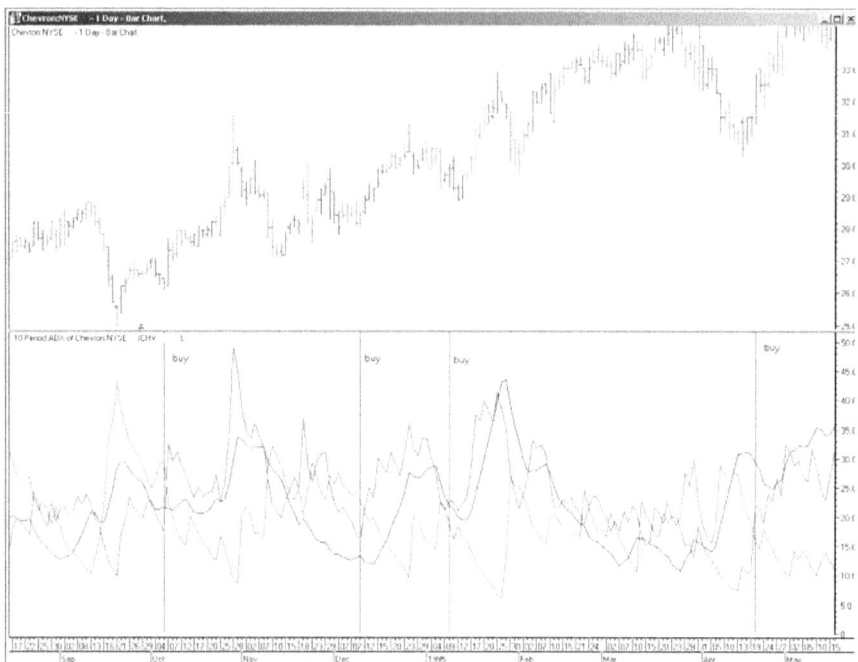

BOLLINGER BANDS

Bollinger Bands are based on a standard moving average. The actual band lines are offset by a positive and negative standard deviation value from the central moving average value, to provide upper and lower bands. For each of the bars, the moving average is first calculated. The offset is then calculated as the standard deviation over the same average calculation. This offset is then applied to get the position of the upper and lower lines for each bar. The bands are then the joining of the upper and lower values for each bar.

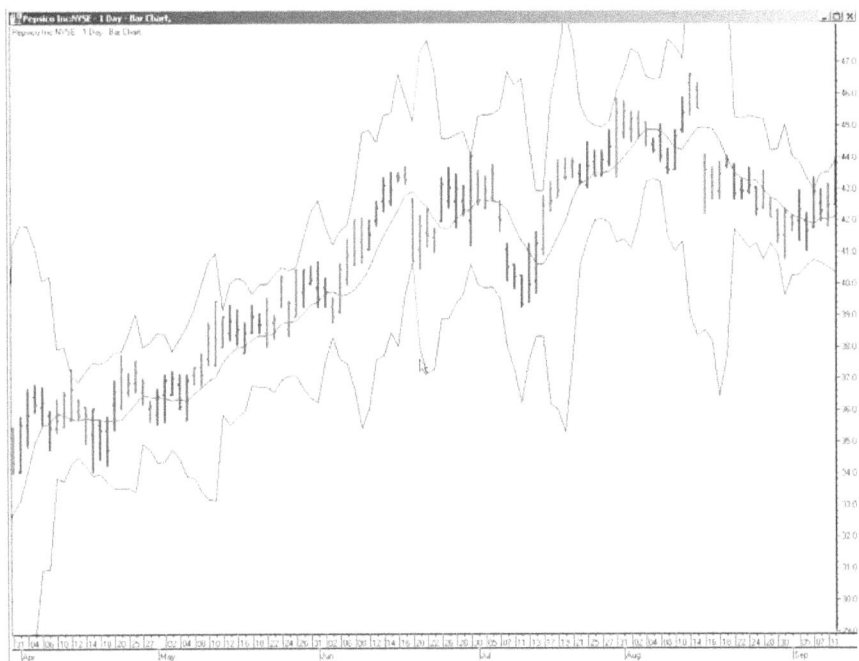

COMMODITY CHANNEL INDEX

Commodity Channel Index (CCI) is used to give a measurement of how far a security is from it's statistical mean. High values mean that the current price is higher than the mean. The calculation is done in the following steps.

For each bar - average the High, Low, and Close.

Calculate a moving average of these values.

For each bar in the calculation, subtract the final bars average (step 2) value from the OHC average calculated in step 1.

Calculate a moving average of the values in step 3.

Multiply the value by 0.015.

Subtract the value given from Step 2 from the value in step 1.

Divide the value in Step 6 by the value in Step 5.

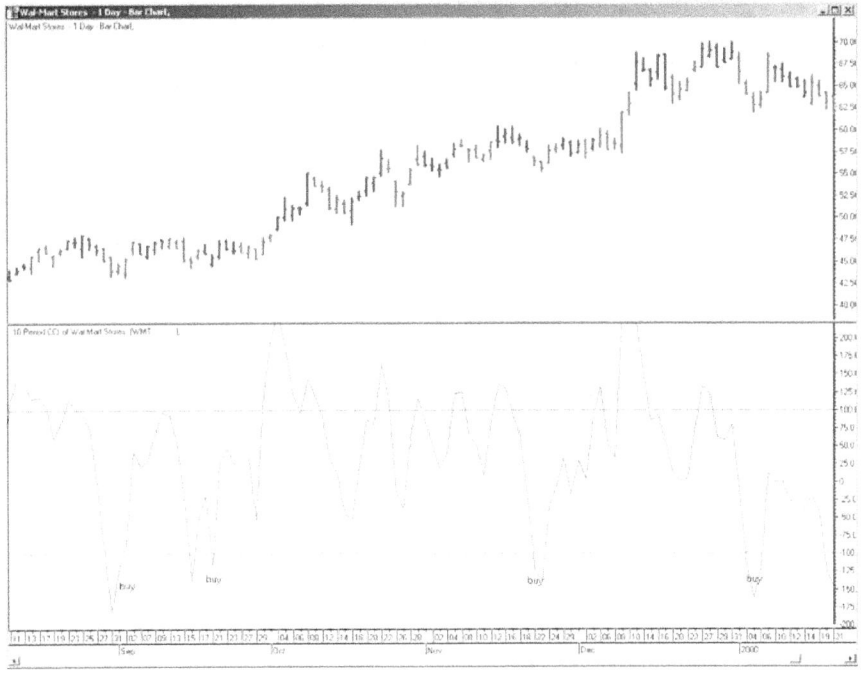

Patterns and Ellipses

KELTNER CHANNELS

Channels are based on a standard moving average. The actual band lines are offset by a positive and negative standard deviation value from the central moving average value, to provide upper and lower bands. For each of the bars, the moving average is first calculated. The average range is then calculated over the same number of bars. The band's values are then calculated as the central average + or - the range average multiplied by a constant.

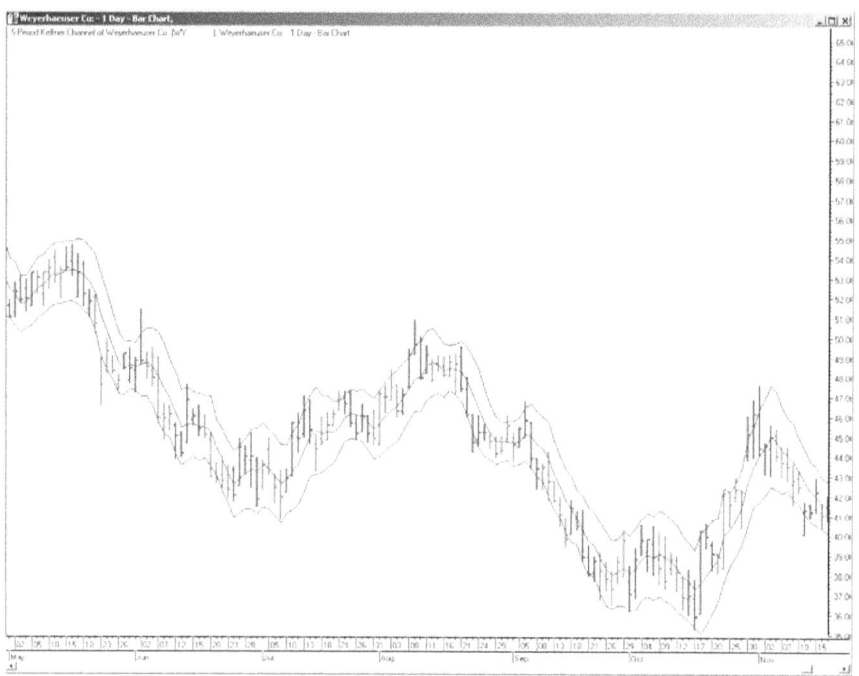

MACD INDICATOR

A MACD (Moving Average Convergence Divergence) is the difference between an Oscillator and a Moving Average of that Oscillator. MACD's are always calculated using exponential Moving Averages based on the close of the bars.

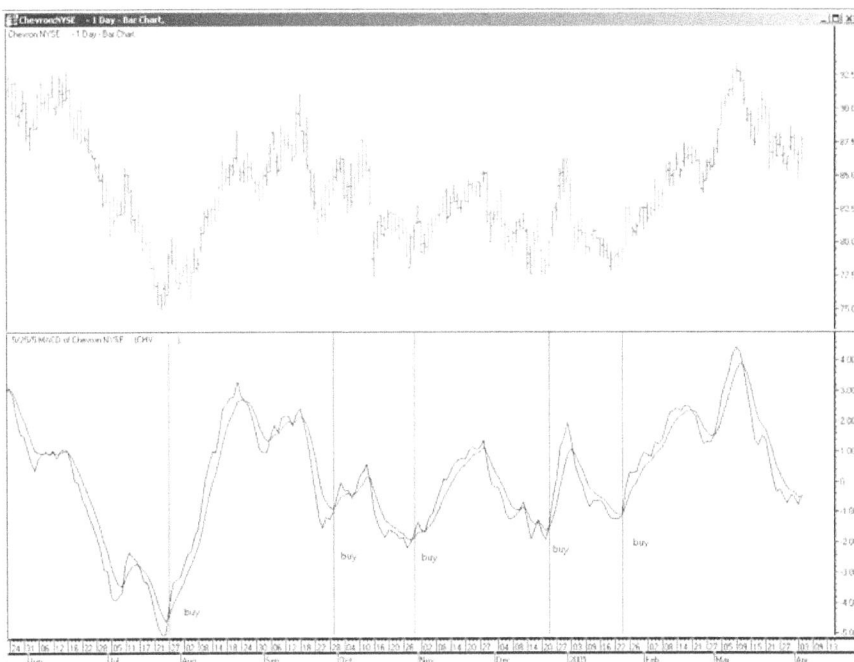

Patterns and Ellipses

MOVING AVERAGE BANDS

Moving Average Bands are based on a standard on a standard moving average. The actual band lines are offset by a positive and negative value from the central moving average value, to provide upper and lower bands. For each of the bars, the moving average is first calculated. The offset is then applied to get the position of the upper and lower lines for each bar. The bands are then the joining of the upper and lower values for each bar. The offset is a percentage of the moving average value.

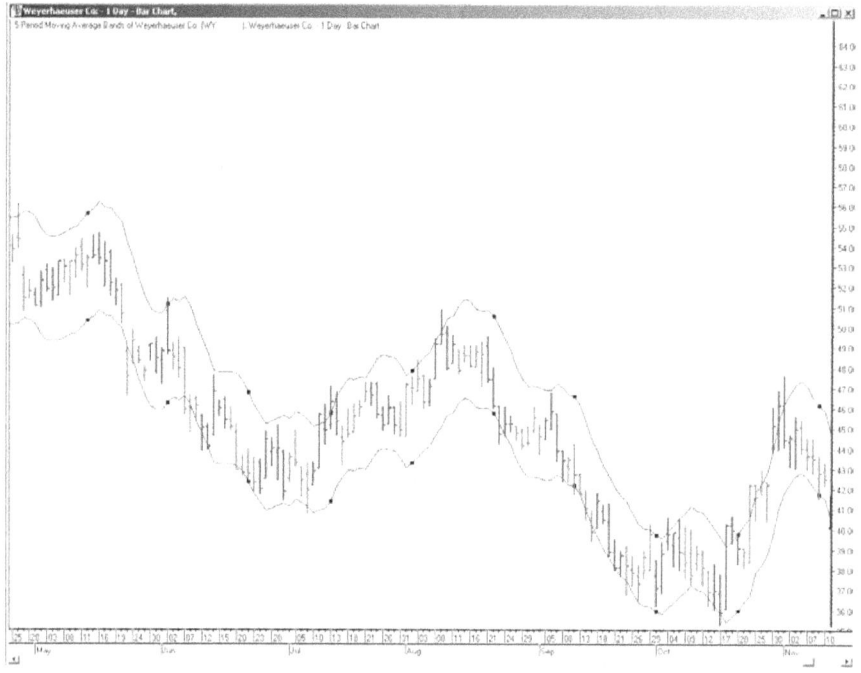

MOVING AVERAGES and CYCLES

Moving averages can be used to give trend direction and even cycles. Displayed here is a 12-day moving average moved to the right 4 days. If the price action makes a high and the moving average shows a turn, then it is considered a short term cycle high. If the price action makes a low and the moving average shows a turn then it is considered a short term cycle low. As for trend changes, if the prices get above a rising moving averages the trend is up and conversely if the prices drop below a falling moving average the price trend is down. See the below chart.

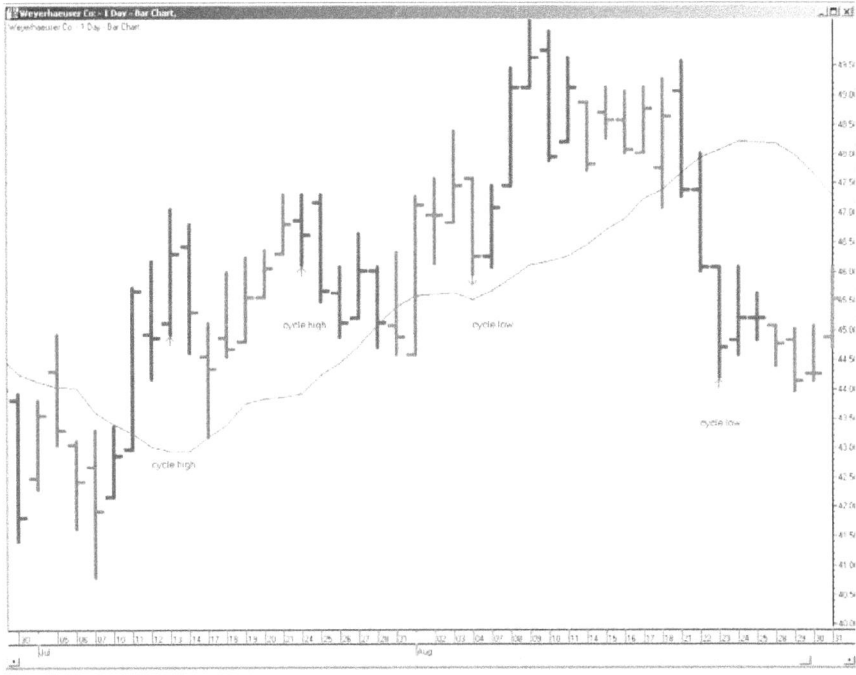

Patterns and Ellipses

MOVING AVERAGE MOMENTUM

Moving average momentum can be used to give you a clearer change of trend indication. Looking at the chart below, we have set the Moving Average Momentum at 12. When the oscillator gets at the top and crosses a trend line, it is a short-term sell. Conversely when the Moving Average Momentum gets to the bottom and it crosses a trend line it is a buy.

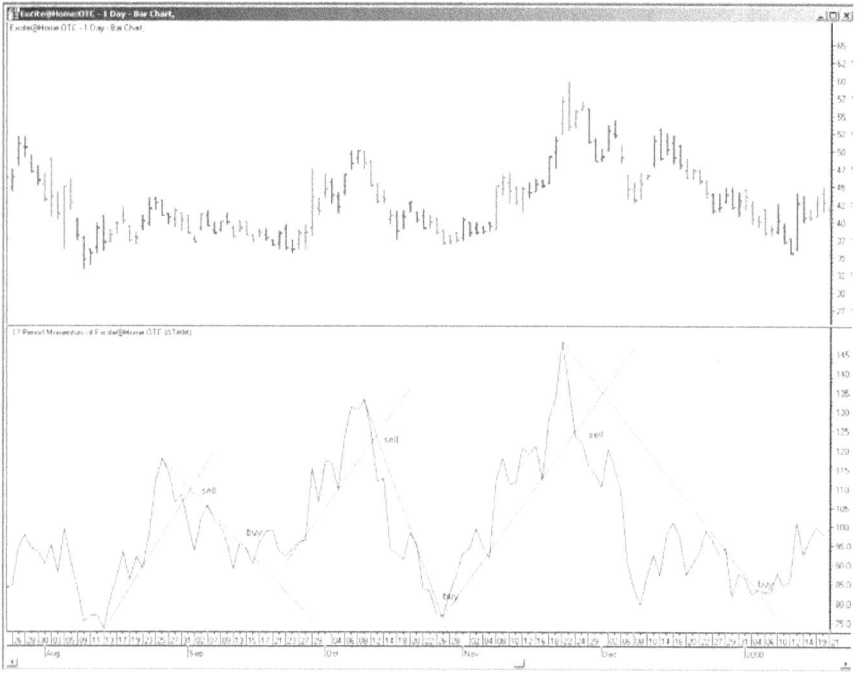

PARABOLIC STOP AND REVERSE

The Parabolic Stop and Reverse (P-SAR) indicator derives it name from the fact that when applied it resembles a parabola. The P-SAR has basically been designed to set price stops.

The P-SAR is calculated as follows:

SARTomorrow = SARToday + AF(EPTrade − SARToday)

Where:

SAR = Stop and Reverse

AF = Acceleration Factor

EP = Extreme Price

The SAR stop level value is drawn on the day in which it is in effect.

Below is an illustration of the Parabolic Stop and Reverse System. It can be used effectively with occasional short-term losses and whipsaws. Many traders use it more in conjunction with other method of trading.

Patterns and Ellipses

5/25 PRICE OSCILLATOR

This is the famous 5/25 Price Oscillator that Tom Joseph uses on his expensive Elliott Wave Program. If you learn to recognize the pattern of this price oscillator you can easily determine were you are in the classical Elliott Wave pattern of waves.

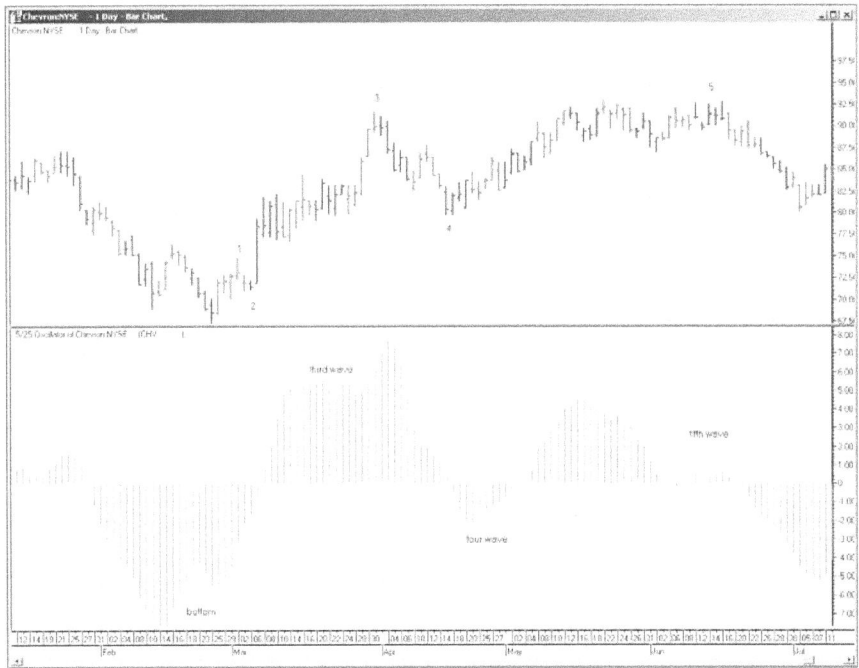

Patterns and Ellipses

RATE OF CHANGE

Rate of Change (ROC) is used to give a measurement of the momentum of a security. High values indicate that the security is increasing in price rapidly, low values indicate the price is falling rapidly. The ROC is calculated by subtracting the closing price n bars ago from today's price. The value is then displayed as a percentage.

((Today's Close - Close n bars ago)/Close n bars ago) x 100

This oscillator works excellent with divergence. When the bottom Rate of Change Oscillator shows loss of momentum and the top prices are still advancing you can usually make a trade with the 2 to 3 bump on the oscillator.

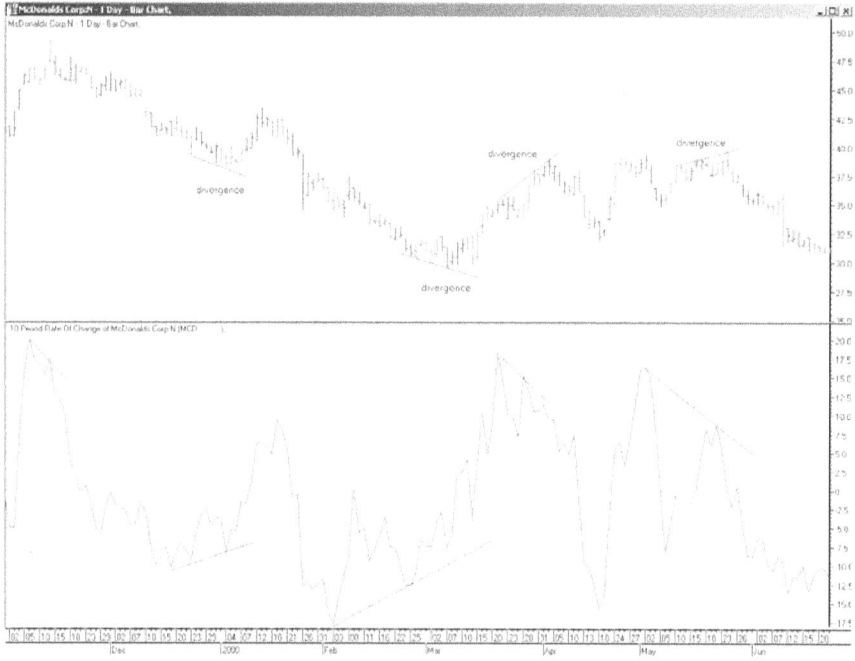

138

RELATIVE STRENGTH INDEX

Relative Strength Index (RSI) is an oscillator that follows price movement. All the values where the close is above the previous close are added together, and all those below are added, giving a total UP value and a total DOWN value. The RSI is then calculated as:

RSI = 100 - (100/(1 + (Up / Down))

The Relative Strength Index is somewhat like the Rate of Change Oscillator. It many times gives you divergence at the tops and bottoms of trends. It is best not to rely on this oscillator alone, but to use other signals as confirmation.

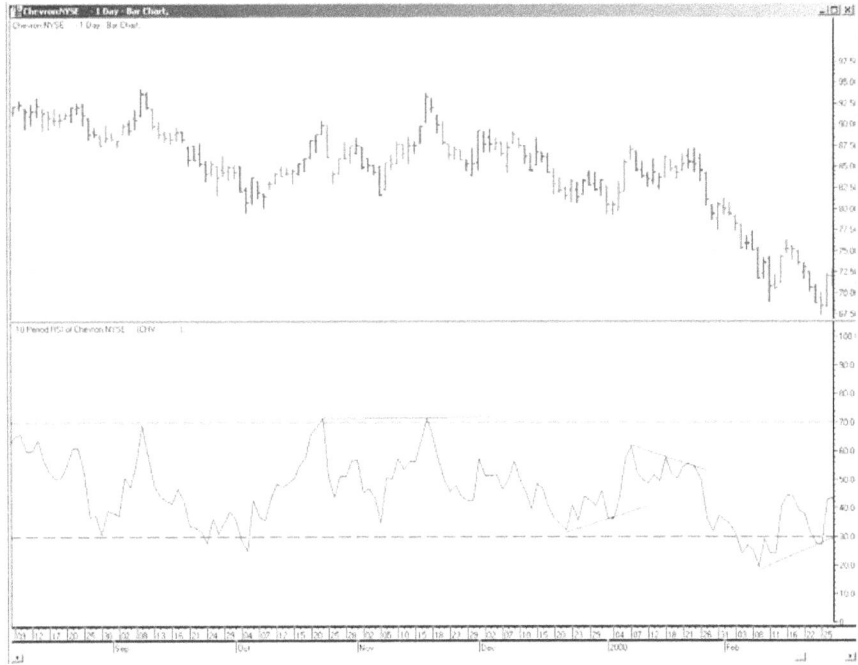

Patterns and Ellipses

STOCHASTICS

Stochastics is an oscillator that is displayed as two lines. The first line, %K, is the main stochastic calculation. The second, %D, is a moving average of %K. A Slow Stochastic simply uses the %D line as the %K line and calculates a new moving average of the %K(old %D) as the new %D line. First the %K value is calculated.

%D is calculated as a moving average of %K.

To use the system effectively try to buy when the market is in an uptrend and the oscillator is near 20 and has a crossover. Here again as with all oscillators, its best to use it with another set of confirming indicators or tools.

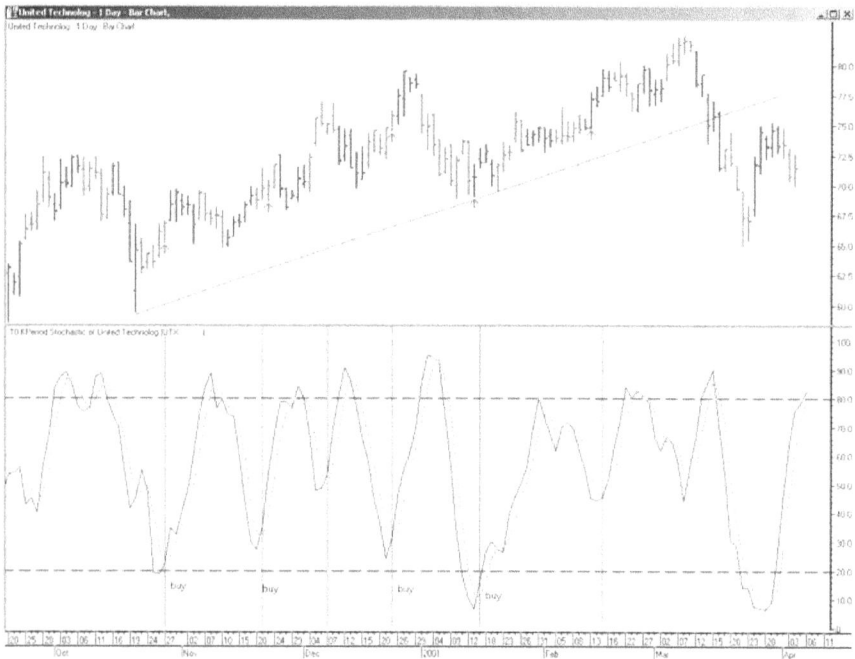

Larry Jacobs

TEMPERATURE

Temperature is an oscillator that follows price movement. It follows certain rules to give values of 5 to -5.

The rules for the temperature chart are as follows.

Set Result to 0.

if Today's Close > Yesterday's Close

Add 2 to the Result.

if Today's Close < Yesterday's Close

Subtract 2 from the Result.

if Today's Open < Today's Close

Add 2 to the Result.

if Today's Open > Today's Close

Subtract 2 from the Result.

if Today's low > Yesterday's Close

Add 1 to the Result.

if Today's High < Yesterday's Close

Subtract 1 from the Result

This is a very short-term oscillator. When the oscillator gets to the center in a down-trend sell. In an uptrend you should buy when the signal is at the center. Again use this system with other signals for confirmation of buy or sell signals.

Patterns and Ellipses

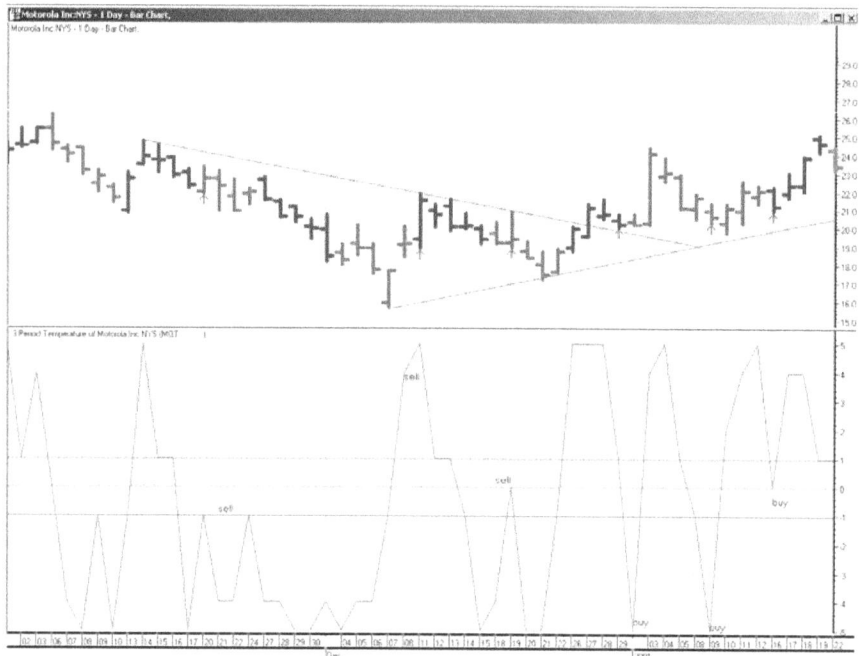

WILLIAMS %R

Williams %R (WR) is a momentum indicator developed by Larry Williams that measures overbought and oversold levels. The calculation is similar to the stochastic oscillator.

This is an excellent oscillator to use for short-term trading. Can be used effectively with trend lines to determine quick trading signals.

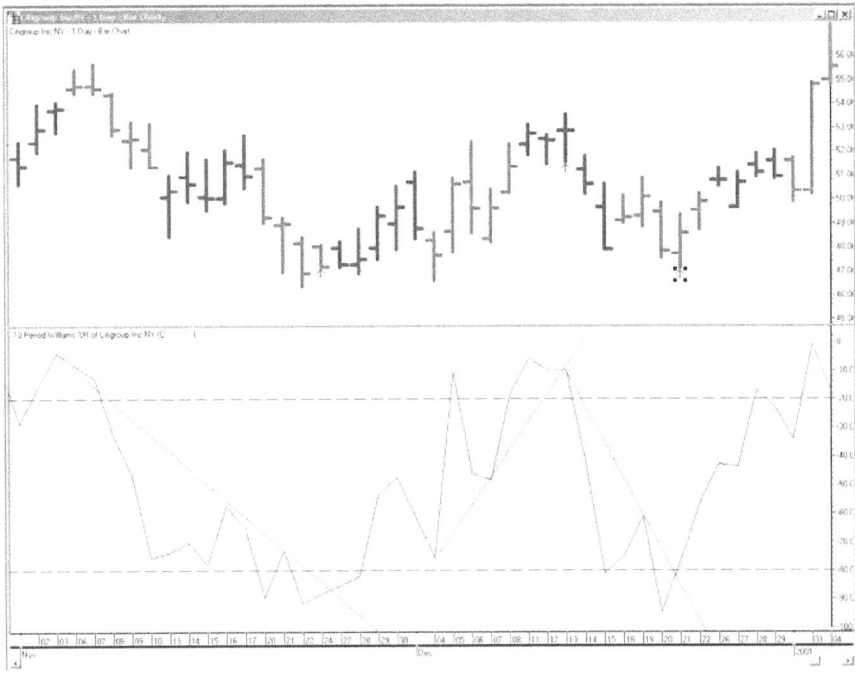

Patterns and Ellipses

Larry Jacobs

LINEAR REGRESSION

Linear Regression (LR) is a statistical method for finding the "line of best fit". Given a set of points, the least squares method is used to calculate a line that best sums up the trend of the market. LR's use a complex statistical calculation called Least Squares Method to calculate the line of best fit. It is beyond the scope of this manual to go into detail of that calculation.

With the excellent center best fit trend line given by Linear Regression you can effectively produce parallel trend lines at the top for taking profits in an uptrend or at the bottom to determine if a market has broken its main trend and to sell on the first reaction. See chart below.

Patterns and Ellipses

HISTORICAL VOLATILITY RATIO

The Historical Volatility Ratio can be used to determine when a market is going to become active. In the below example the market of Caterpillar Tractor was moving sideways in a narrow ban. The Historical Volatility Ratio was declining with a clear trend line down. When the ratio broke out on the upside a change of trend was forecasted. A trend line could then be drawn on the latest price trend on the stock and sold on the first reaction as indicated below.

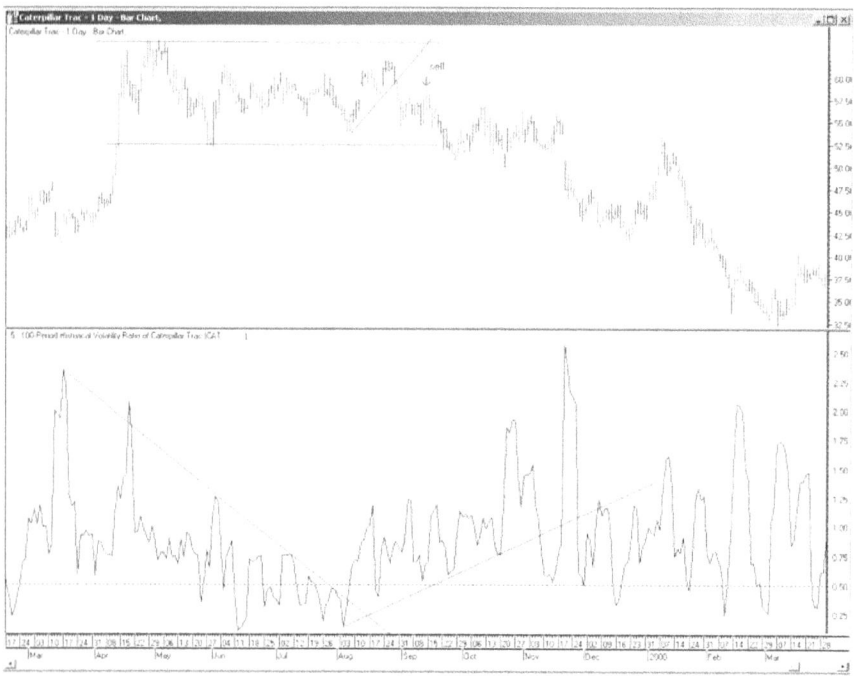

STANDARD DEVIATION

Standard Deviation (SD) can be used to measure volatility. It is normally used with other indicators but can also be used on it's own. SD's are calculated by finding the simple moving average over n bars, then summing the squares of the difference between the data item and the moving average for each of the n bars. This sum is divided by n and the square root is calculated. This oscillator can be used as an divergent indicator of tops and bottoms. You can buy on the trend line breaks of the Standard Deviation Oscillator when you have clear divergence at the top.

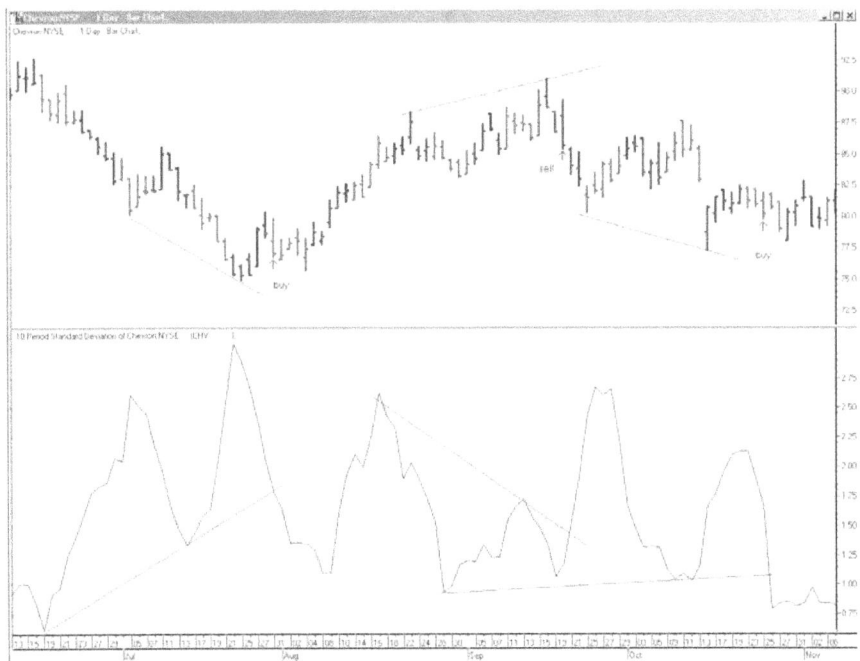

VOLUME ADVANCE DECLINE OSCILLATOR

The Volume Advance Decline Oscillator can be used with a trend line. The trend line usually forms after the bottom and has usually 3 or more touches. Once broken you can look to make a trade in the market waiting for the first reaction.

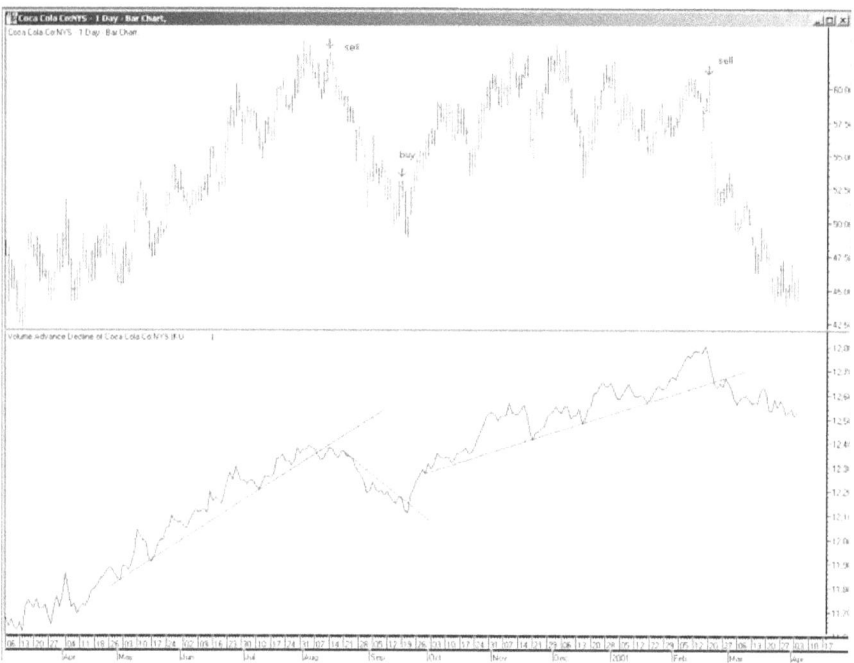

MIDAS INDICATOR

The Midas (MDS) indicator was developed by Paul Levine. Midas is an acronym for Marketing Interpretation/Data Analysis System. This system is designed to focus on the dynamic interplay of support/resistance and accumulation/distribution in determining price behavior. A Midas chart can clarify an otherwise random or chaotic market.

In the following chart we used it to indicate a major down trend. Reactions against the main trend could be sold using the indicator after it dropped under the reaction support.

MONEY FLOW INDEX

Money Flow Index (MFI) is a similar indicator to the RSI, but the MFI uses volume to measure the strength of the money flowing in and out of the security.

The calculation is done in the following steps.

1. For each bar, average the High, Low, and Close.

2. The MF value is equal to the Average x Volume.

3. If the value in step 1 is higher than the previous, it is considered to be a positive money value, otherwise negative. The positive money flow is then the sum of all the positive money values over the number of bars.

4. The money ratio is then + MF divided by -MF.

5. The Index is then 100 - (100 / (1 + Money Ratio)).

This oscillator can be used like the RSI indicator. It display divergence and high levels at 70 on the scale can be generally sold in a downtrend. In an up trend the levels of 30 could be bought. Use it with confirming indicators.

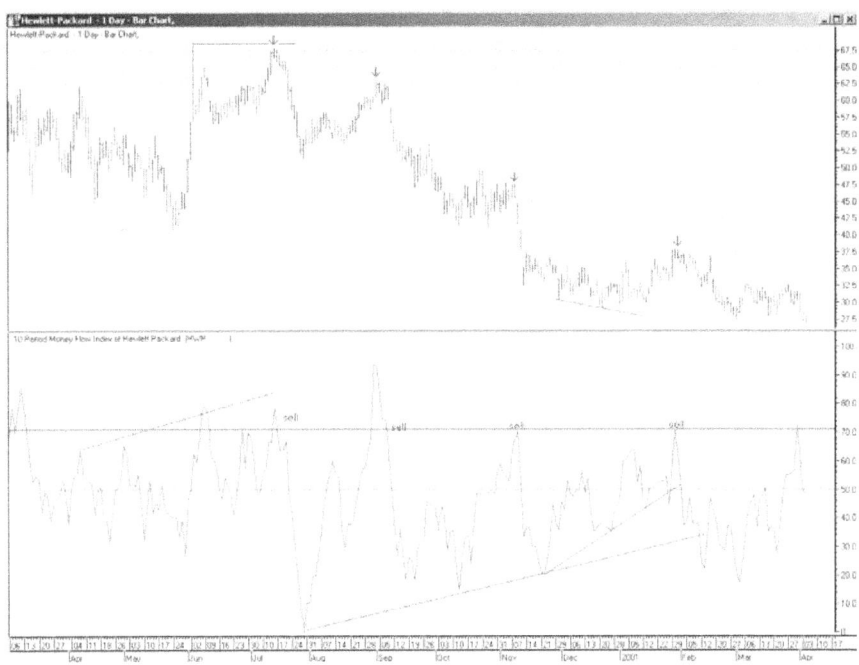

OPEN INTEREST

Open Interest (OI) is used to depict the number of contracts outstanding, i.e. the number of contracts that must be settled before the expiry date of the commodity. Not all data files have OI.

In a downtrend rising OI is bearish. New shorts are entering the market.

In an uptrend rising OI is bullish. New longs are entering the market.

In a downtrend falling OI is bullish. Shorts are liquidating.

In an uptrend fall OI is bearish. Longs are liquidating out of the market.

In the below example with rising OI in the downtrend a sell was given when we broke the upward reaction line on the left of the chart. A buy was finally given on the right side of the chart when OI began to rise and the downward trend line broke.

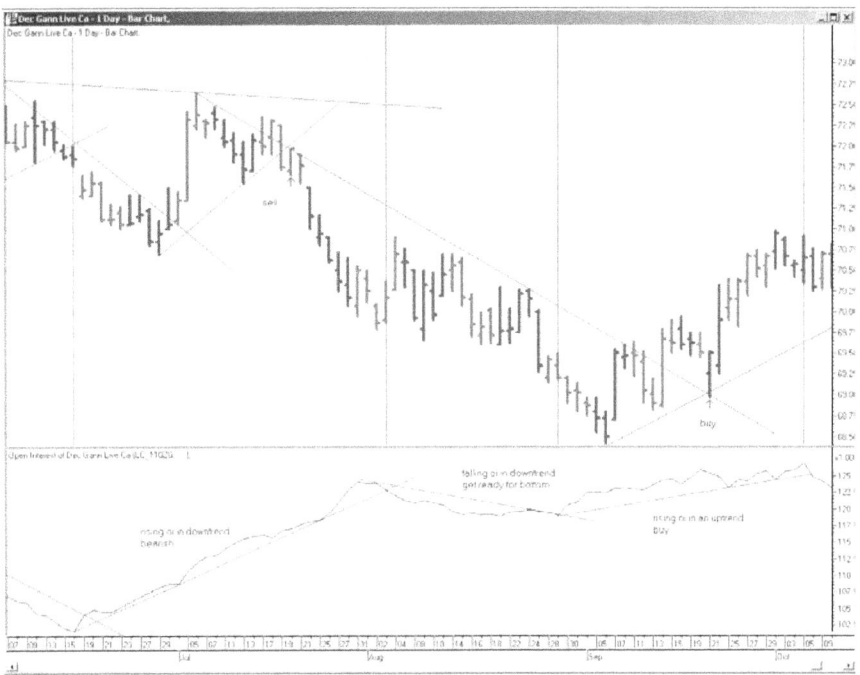

ON BALANCE VOLUME

On Balance Volume (OBV) is an oscillator, which relates price movement to volume.

The OBV is a cumulative summation based on certain criteria. They are as follows:

If today's close is greater than yesterday's close

OBV = Yesterday's OBV + Today's Volume.

If today's close is less than yesterday's close

OBV = Yesterday's OBV - Today's Volume.

If today's close is the same as yesterday's close

OBV = Yesterday's OBV.

In the below example when OBV is in a downtrend sell all rallies and when it's in an uptrend buy all reactions.

Patterns and Ellipses

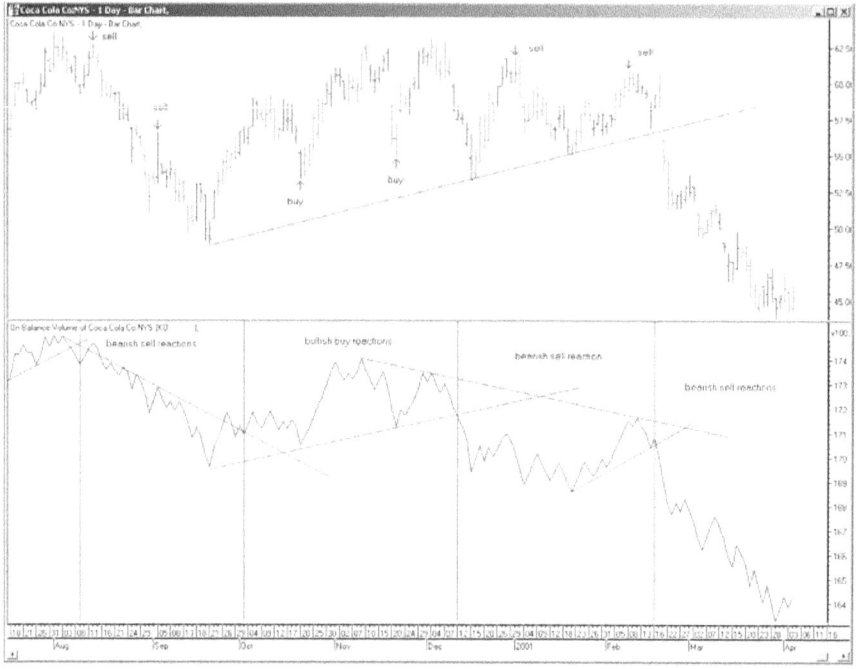

ON BALANCE VOLUME %

As per On Balance Volume however the scale is calculated as a %.

As the previous example with OBV use the same strategy when OBV% is in an uptrend buy all reactions and when OBV% is in a downtrend sell all rallies.

Larry Jacobs

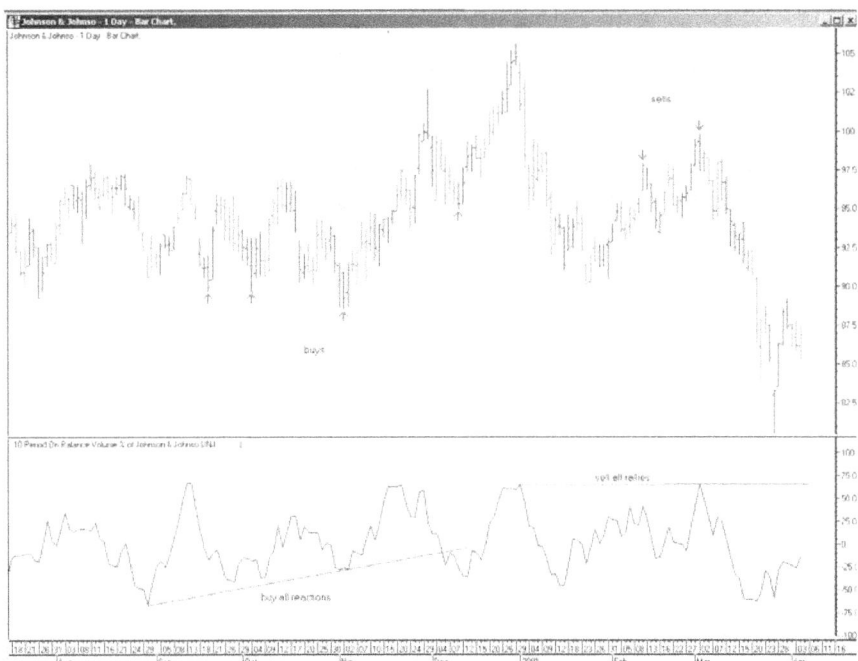

Patterns and Ellipses

VOLUME

Volume is important as it confirms the direction of the move. A rising trend should have rising volume and a falling trend should have falling volume to have a bullish market. Conversely a bearish trend has rising volume in a falling market and falling volume on a rising market.

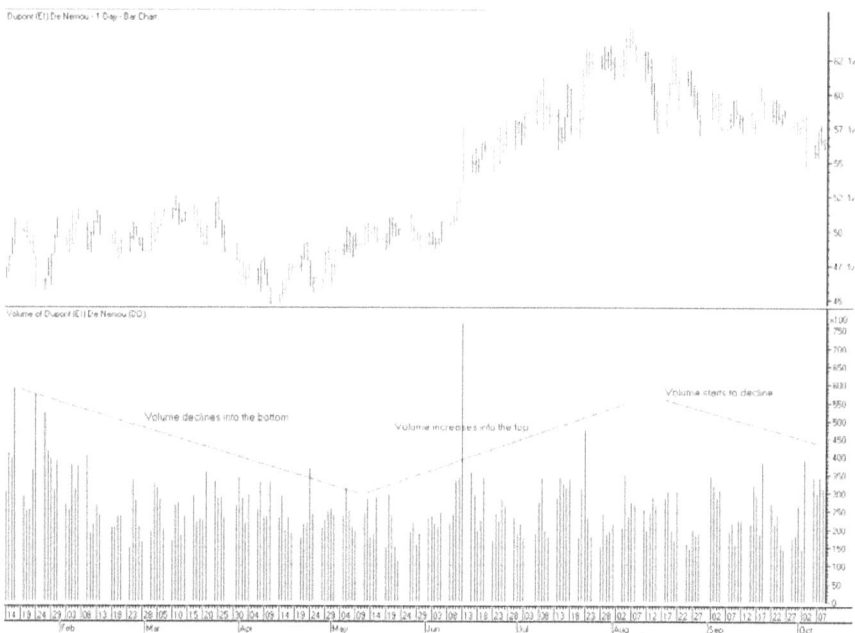

PRICE MOVES

Previously we indicated that all stocks and commodities move within certain price moves. See the following.

35*.25 = 8.75

35*.375= 13.125

35*.5 = 17.5

35*.625 = 21.875

35*.75 = 26.25

35*.875 = 30.625

35*1 = 35

35*2= 70

35*2.5=122

Look at the following chart of Dupont that we have been working with and you will see that the first move A approximately 13.125 points, B equaled 8.75 points, C = 21.875 points and from the bottom to the top 26.25 points. If you add up A, B and C point moves you get the magical number of 35! See the following chart.

Patterns and Ellipses

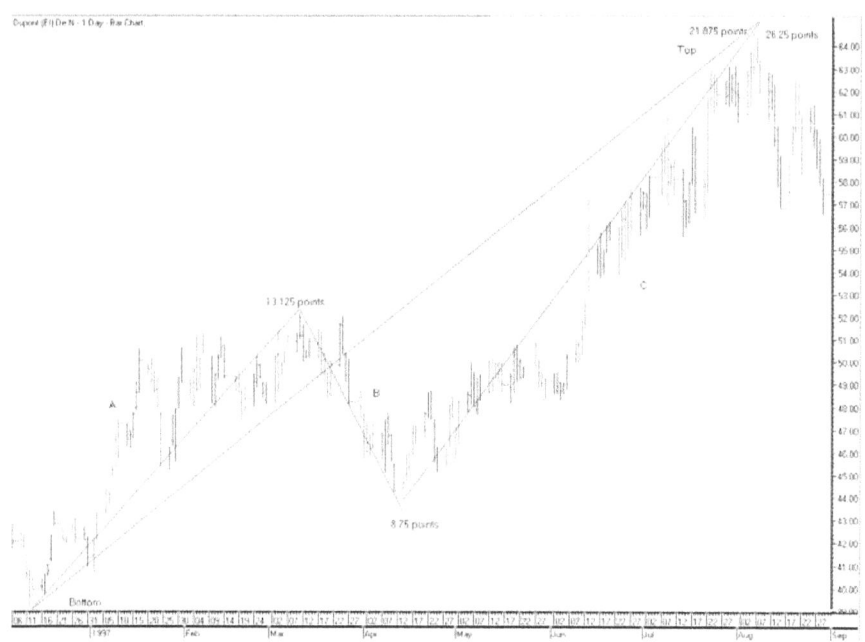

Larry Jacobs

GAPS

A gap is an open space on your charts between one trading day and another. Gaps usually are something that is nothing to think about. In fact most gaps are usually closed within 1 to 3 days. Some gaps are closed several days or weeks later. Some traders use them as objectives. An open gap is many times a target for a potential move. See the following chart.

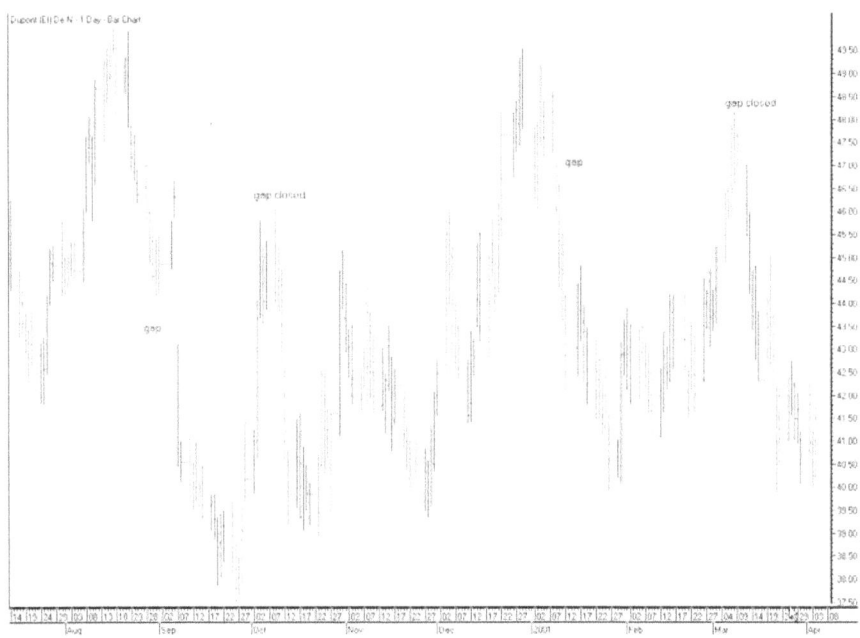

When a gap occurs with velocity, it is something to watch. It's called a breakaway gap. In most cases it is the beginning of an accelerated move. The top or the bottom then must be considered as in place. The move does not start from that top or bottom but from the gap. The move starts from the bottom of the gap in a downtrend and the top of a gap in a uptrend. The move will last one of these numbers:

35*.25 = 8.75

35*.375= 13.125

Patterns and Ellipses

35*.5 = 17.5

35*.625 = 21.875

35*.75 = 26.25

35*.875 = 30.625

35*1 = 35

35*2= 70

35*2.5=122

See the gaps on the below chart. They both started off with a bang and continued strong and made one of the numbers above.

OTHER GAPS

The other types of gaps are the midpoint gap and the exhaustion gap. The midpoint gap occurs after a move has started. In the middle of the move it makes an open gap. From that point you can measure in the middle of the gap and project a measured move. In the following chart you see an example of a midpoint gap, which projected to an exact top. Later on you also see an exhaustion gap that terminated the move of the stock. See the chart below.

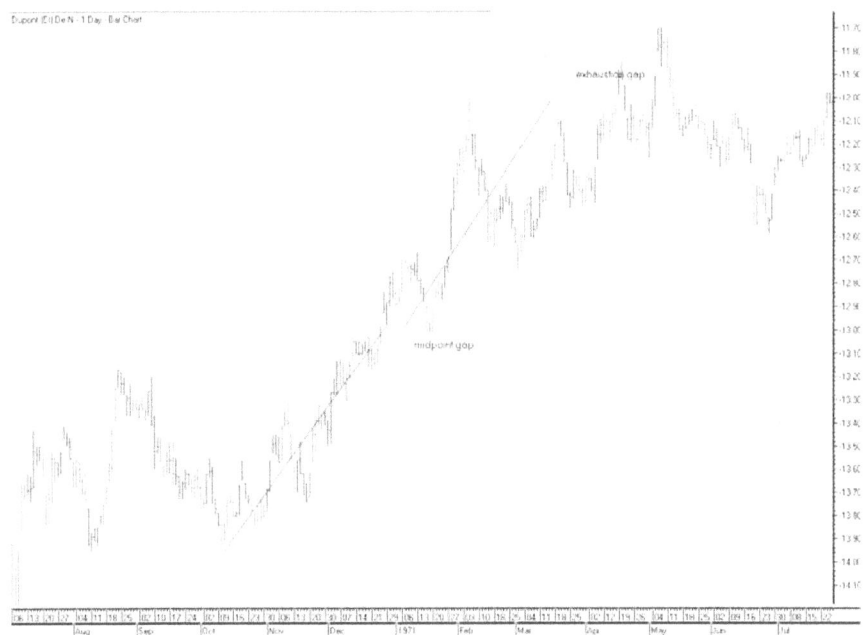

Patterns and Ellipses

ELLIPSES

There are many mathematicians in the world. Most of them understand what mathematical equations make up the ellipse and how it works. Very few of them know that stocks and commodities move in fixed ellipses. By experimenting with ellipses there are a few numbers that work nicely. You must experiment to find one that works with an individual market. Two ellipses normally work with a market. A large ellipse is normally used for a primary move and a smaller one is used for a reactionary move. The sizes of ellipses are usually 6, 9, 12, 15 and 18 ratios to each other. The movement is not over until the market breaks out of the ellipse. The market is almost like a gold fish in a bowl. Once it's there it's almost impossible to escape unless it gets out with a gap. The beginning of an ellipse is usually within a previous ellipse. You need at lease two points to start a new ellipse. In the following example we have 3 points A, B and C. Notice how the prices move and touch the outer edge and the axis of the ellipse. This gives you the direction of the move that can be expected. You need at least 5 points to put the ellipse in the right direction. See the chart below.

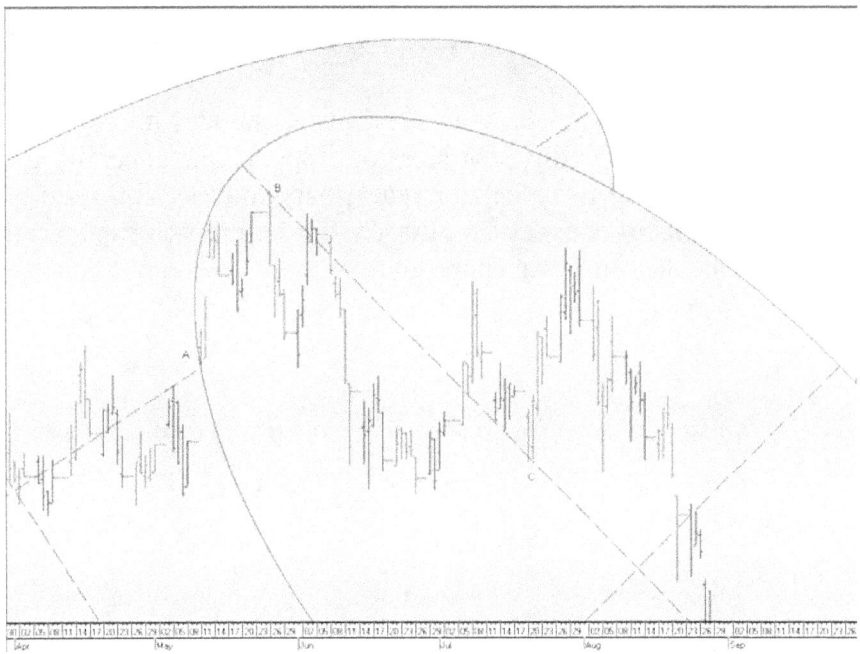

DIFFERENT SIZES OF ELLIPSES

In the following example you see how General Motors stock moved within the two different sizes of ellipses. One generally for impulse moves and the other for reactionary moves. You need at least five points to consider an ellipse valid before you can start a new one. See the following chart.

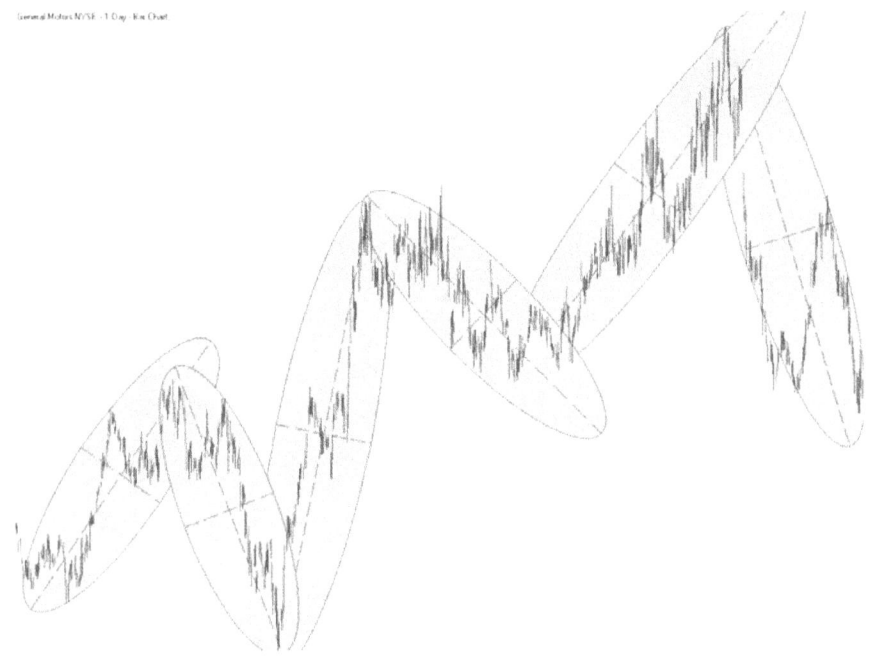

CHANNELS WITH ELLIPSES

Many markets will move with ellipses, which are connected together. The ellipses actually form a channel by themselves. Trend lines can even be placed on these channels. When the channel is broken by price action the trend is over. The trader should then be looking for signs of a new emerging trend.

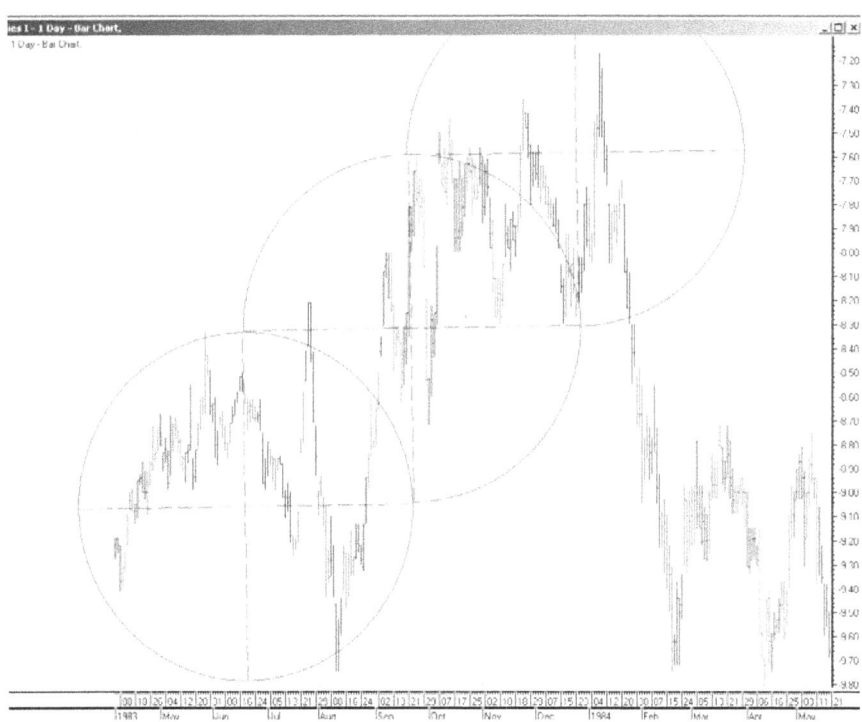

CHANNELS WITH ELLIPSES – CHANGE OF TREND

Looking at the chart below you can see that a change of trend occurred when the primary channel of ellipses was broken. Look how the new channel forms after the downward breakout.

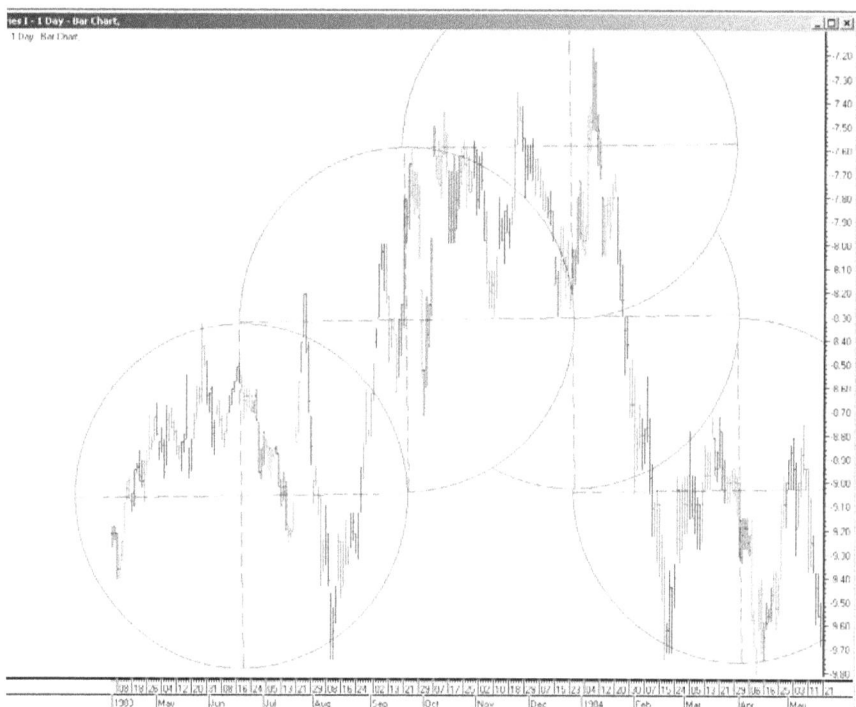

Larry Jacobs

SIDEWAYS TRENDING CHANNEL

The following is an illustration of just a sideways trending chart formed with ellipses. You can clearly see how the ellipses fit with the price action of this chart.

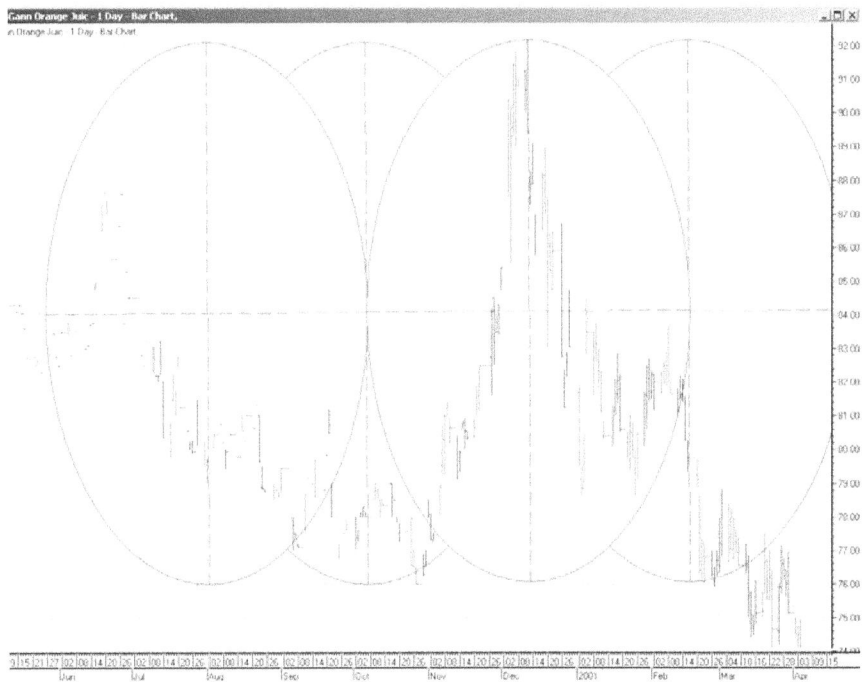

Patterns and Ellipses

CHANGE OF DIRECTION CHANNEL

This example shows how price action changed directions from an upward move to a downward move. The action toward the bottom of the chart shows a decline and loss of momentum.

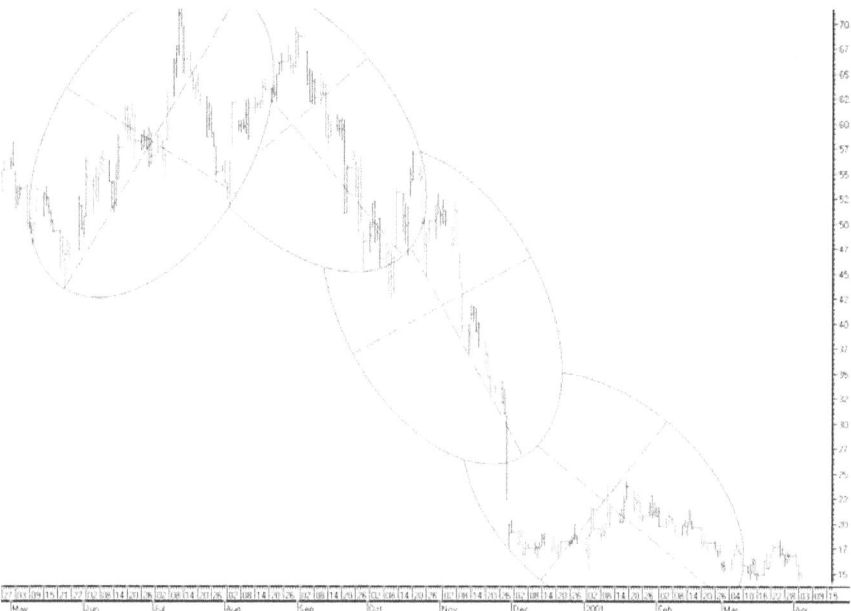

Larry Jacobs

FORMATIONS – EGG OF COLUMBUS

George Bayer was a famous market trader, course and newsletter writer in the 1940's. He felt it was his job was to teach those interested in how to trade the markets with strange, innate but accurate cycles. He felt that writers such as Swedenborg who had written 20,000 pages and Athenaeus who had written some 3000 pages had just scratched the surface of cycle study. He wanted to condense the study of cycles down to just a very few pages but make every page count and mean a lot. He wrote several courses and a series of newsletters.

He also felt that the people living ages ago were much smarter and wiser than anyone living in his time. He felt that he got his wisdom from studying them. He said that he didn't owe his generation a nickel's worth of thanks. He even said the current generation held him back; having to wade through all their works until his hard thinking put him on the right tract.

He felt that the forecast of what is to come, for example, in wheat or corn next year was preset and continuing. To be successful all one had to do was to try to locate the cycle and ride with it. He felt this was extremely difficult to do for the average person. He felt that each living creature on earth has its own cycle it was living in. This cycle may or may not be harmonious with the cycles of other living things. He felt that if someone's own cycle was disharmonious with stocks or commodities that person will never want to trade in them. Others whose cycles are harmonious with stocks will trade them and win.

He felt that traders get vaccinated with false opinions as to what moves the markets. This comes from newspapers, books written on the subject of market analysis and today even television. Look at CNBC. It clearly and constantly bombards the public with it's opinions and the opinions of its guests. The ideas and opinions of these people are imbedded into the minds of the public and it's almost impossible to get these ideas out of their minds. The public thinks they know what affects the market. For example frost in

Patterns and Ellipses

Iowa or rain in Kansas moves wheat up and down.

In his course the Egg of Columbus, George Bayer brings up the study of Athenaeus and his study of cycles. There is a natural law which says: you'll get what is coming to you and you never will get that which is not meant for you and therefore you should be able to see quickly how marvelous nature shows itself in all things. He felt that it must be very clear that there is an interweaving of cycles. The secrets contained in Athenaeus could be written with one word or one title: Dinner Table.

He said that what can be understood from the knowledge of cycles is that the cycles of markets, of business, the life of a human being, bank accounts, trading accounts, wheat, cotton, and every commodity consists of a series of cycles, long and short, which form one whole. Links form a chain. He called these cycles serpents. The formation of these serpents is represented in things which we eat and in the rotation how we eat the various foods. He said you would not start with the roast when eating a seven-course dinner, but you begin with the Hors d'Oeuvre or Antipasto, that is with radishes, green onions, pickles, salami, anchovies, and caviar. He felt that the Dinner Table was not his ideas, but what the Ancients had known thoroughly. He felt that knowing the theory of the Dinner Table we had to know something about eating and the series in which the dishes of food were served at dinner. There is a definite sequence of how dinner should be served.

Here is the sequence of how food should be served at dinner:

1) Begin with the Hors d'Oeuvre and a cocktail

2) Next follows the soup

3) After the soup comes the fish

4) Small round boiled potatoes are served with the fish.

5) White wine is served with the fish.

Larry Jacobs

6) When the fish as been eaten, we start with the roast

7) With the roast goes red wine.

8) After the roast comes the sweet stuff

9) With it should be served Champagne

10) Then we get cheese and crackers

11) Lastly we get almonds and nuts with which goes a little brandy.

He felt that not only do we have to know about how we eat dinner but also we must know about how the dinner must be disposed of.

Another important point about cycles that George Bayer brought out is that there is an interweaving of cycles. Those who work with ellipses know that the new cycle has to be set within the end of the old ellipse. Fixed stars form distinct pictures of animals in the evening sky. These animals are running around the globe in millions. They eventually die. Don't forget that these animals perpetuate themselves throughout time. A new baby animal is born and then a parent dies later. In other words a new cycles starts before the old one ends. Please remember this important point.

Thus what Mr. Bayer discovered is that all the markets represent full a man who lives, eats and disposes of waste matter. He felt this was an extremely important secret that he rediscovered. Mr. Bayer felt that the sooner you work your mind in to understanding such a menu and go over the various dishes and their sequence the better you will understand the cycles of the markets. The market lives on food, not food as such but pictures of food arranged in the form of a top-notch meal, which includes wine and champagne.

Therefore Mr. Bayer said that if you take any bar chart all you do is look for the Hors d' Oeuvre, then for the soup, afterwards for the fish and its fins, then for the roasted bird with its neck sticking out and even its beak from which it spits out a nut or an almond, then you have gone through the complete bull phase. You know the bull

Patterns and Ellipses

phase is over because he has to get rid of that what he has eaten and begins first to p—and then to s—and he repeats that several times, in fact he does this so often until the tongue hands out of his mouth, because he is so hungry that he must eat at once. The handing out of the tongue is the surest sign that he is cleaned from what he had eaten and you will never forget the picture of a tongue if you see one.

Remember Mr. Bayer measured everything with a 6, 9 and ½ of a 6-inch ellipse. This was based on the chart paper he used and the grid per inch. But using this for the basis of his measurement he said the size of the:

1) Tongue is about ½ of a 6-inch ellipse.

2) The fish takes a 6-inch ellipse

3) The bird and the neck takes a 9-inch ellipse.

4) The bird alone takes a 6-inch ellipse.

5) The disposal bear move takes a 6, 9 or even 12 or 18-inch ellipse depending on the size of the dinner whereby the first p. can be a 6-inch ellipse with a comeback of half an ellipse when the hill of s. is make followed by another p. and s. until the intake is thoroughly disposed of.

The size of any move depends upon the size of the tongue that sticks out. In the tongue is contained the Hors d'Oeuvre.

The following illustration is a drawing of exactly how Mr. Bayer thought a dinner course should look.

Larry Jacobs

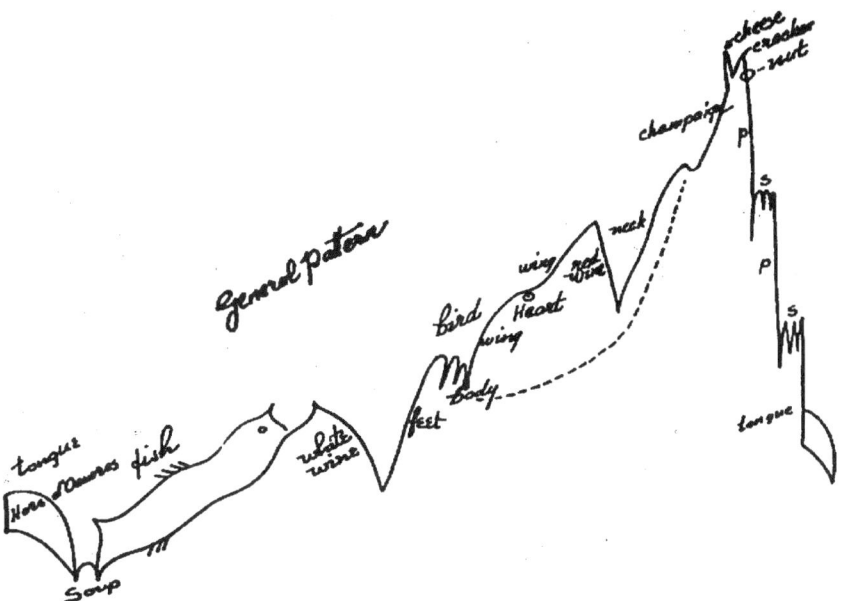

Patterns and Ellipses

EXAMPLE OF DINNER WITH REAL-CHART

The following is an example of how the dinner picture can be used with one of today's charts. Mr. Bayer's pictures of the various parts of the up move are similar to the Elliott Wave Theory. The advantage of Mr. Bayer's methods is that he recognizes each part of the move with pictures of parts of the dinner. He even knows the sizes of the parts of the dinner in relation to the standard ellipses he used.

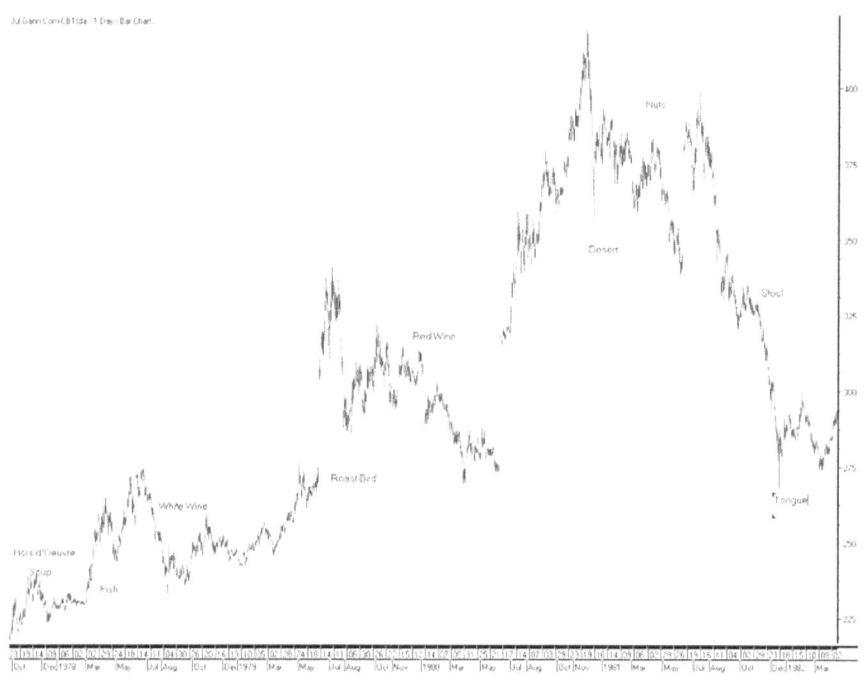

ELLIPSES WORK WITH STANDARD FORMATIONS

We have found that ellipses work in virtually all-standard chart formations. In most cases the ellipses are of the same size. As Mr. Bayer said a new cycle begins before the old one ends. There is an exception to that rule and that is in the area of gaps. Gaps seem to create an entirely new ellipse or a near part of a cycle. In the following chart illustrations of standard formation you will see how we used ellipses. Once you find the ellipse that works you can generally continue to use the same one over and over again. In some cases you might use two sizes of ellipses for chart formation. These chart formations are of minor degrees. After a while you will get used to using the ellipse. It clearly helps you define a chart movement. It also helps you determine when a cycle or movement begins and ends. These ellipses can also be tied to other technical analysis tools such as volume, stochastics, RSI and others.

Patterns and Ellipses

BROADENING BOTTOM FORMATION

In this formation price comes down into an expanding triangle bottom. The formation makes at least 2 higher highs and two lower lows. It must make at least four touches of the triangle. Early on we found the size of the ellipse the market was working in. There are two strategies to use. One strategy is if you recognize the formation early then buy the low at point 5. Put your stop right under the low you bought at. Sell at the top of the triangle at the end of the ellipse or wait for the breakout and sell that the top of the breakout ellipse. The second strategy is to wait for the breakout. Buy immediately and sell at the top of the ellipse. Put your stop under the triangle breakout point.

BROADENING TOP FORMATION

This type of formation is identical to the broadening bottom formation. It needs at least 4 touches of the triangle. The price should eventually breakdown out of the formation and decline. The strategy is to short at point 5 with a close stop, take profits at the bottom of the triangle or wait for the downside breakout and take profits at the bottom of the ellipse. The second strategy would be to wait for the breakout on the downside. Short immediately with a stop inside of the triangle. Then take profits at the bottom of the ellipse.

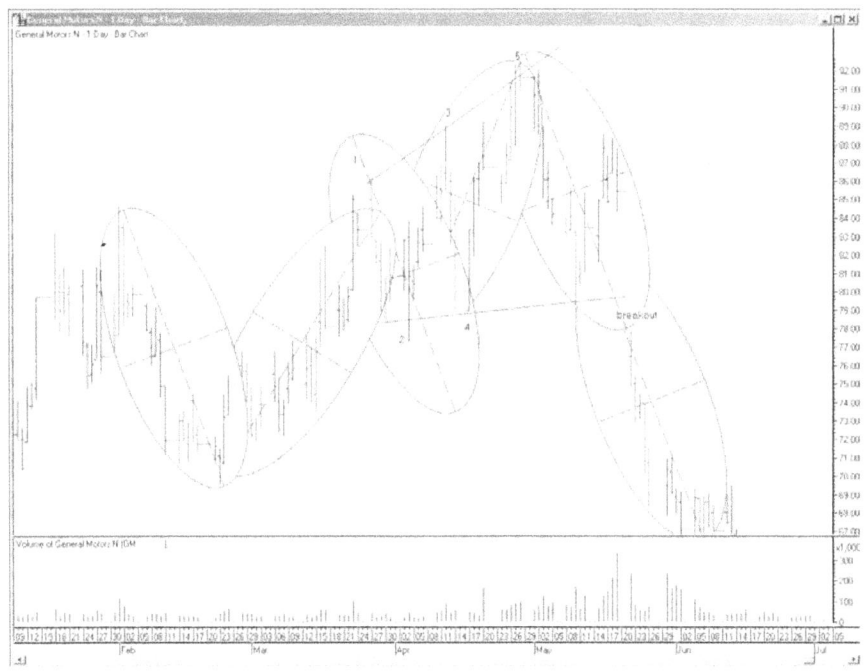

Patterns and Ellipses

RIGHT ANGLE FORMATION

The right angle formation has a flat bottom and a rising angle top. There needs to be at least four touches on the triangle. You can buy at point 5 with a close stop. Take profits at the top of the triangle or wait for it to breakout and take profits at the end of the next ellipse. A second strategy would be to wait for the breakout and then take profits at the end of the next ellipse.

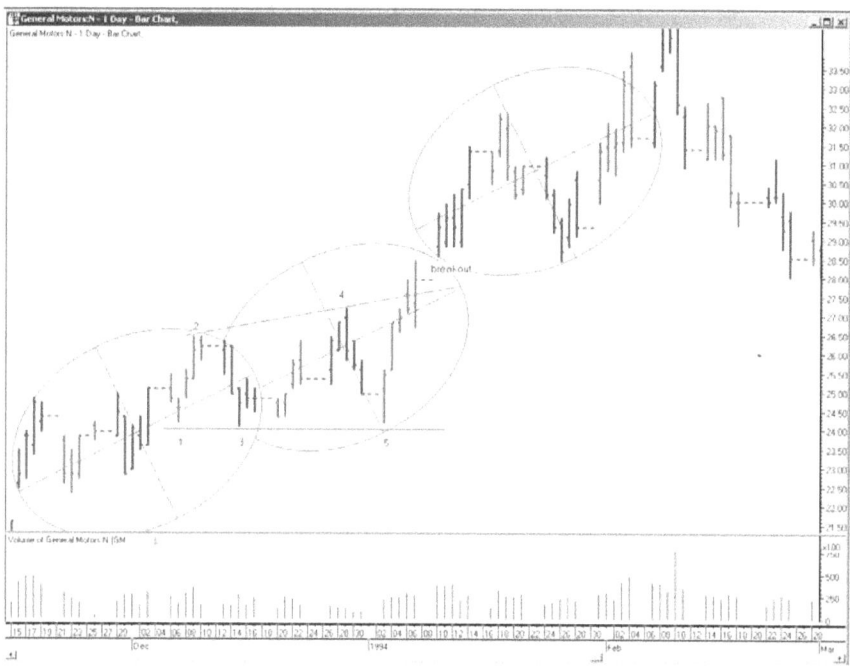

Larry Jacobs

RIGHT ANGLE FORMATION – 5 POINTS TOUCHING

Here is another example of a right hand angle formation with 5 points touching. It's somewhat sloppy compared to the first example. It does however work with the same strategy as the first example. Buy at point 5 or on the breakout and sell at the top of the first ellipse outside of the triangle.

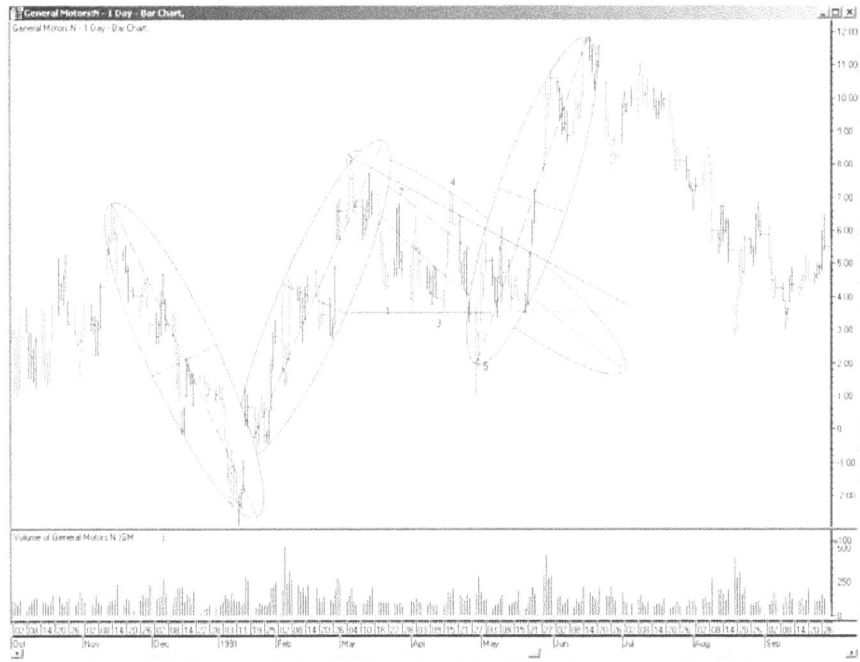

Patterns and Ellipses

RIGHT ANGLE DESCENDING FORMATION

This formation has a flat top and a descending lower angle bottom. Again this triangle must has at least four touch points. Strategy is to buy at point 4 with a close stop. Sell at the top of the triangle. A second strategy would be to sell after the breakout at the top of the ellipse. In this example the market gapped. This is where the bottom of the ellipse was placed according to the rules. With its accelerated move it quickly make the top of the ellipse.

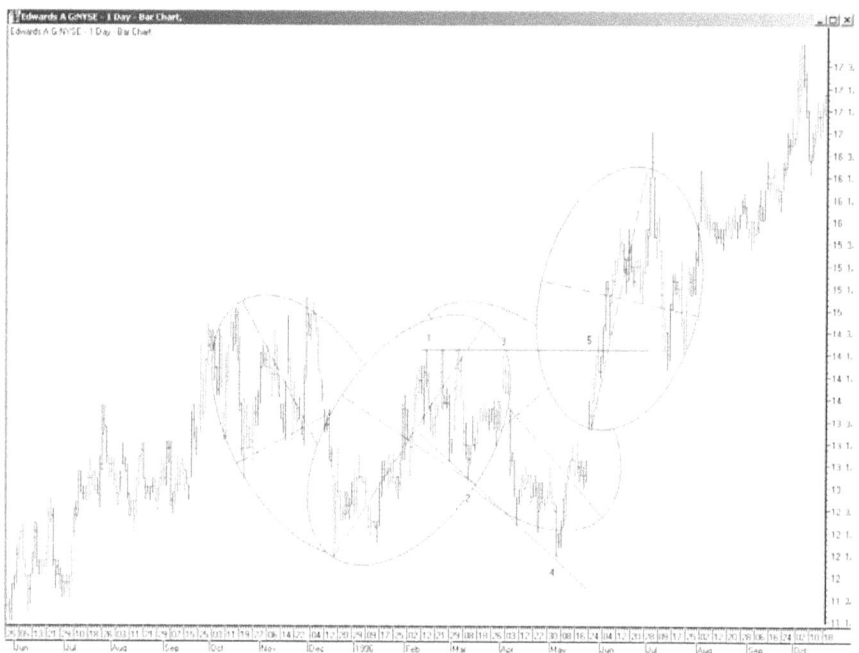

BROADENING ASCENDING WEDGE FORMATION

Here is an example of a broadening ascending wedge formation. Both the top and the bottom slant at an upward angle. There must be at least four touches in the triangle. When it breaks down it usually falls rapidly. Strategy is to sell at the top of the ellipse in the wedge near point 5. You can also sell when it breaks down out of the triangle. Take profits at the bottom of the ellipse outside of the triangle.

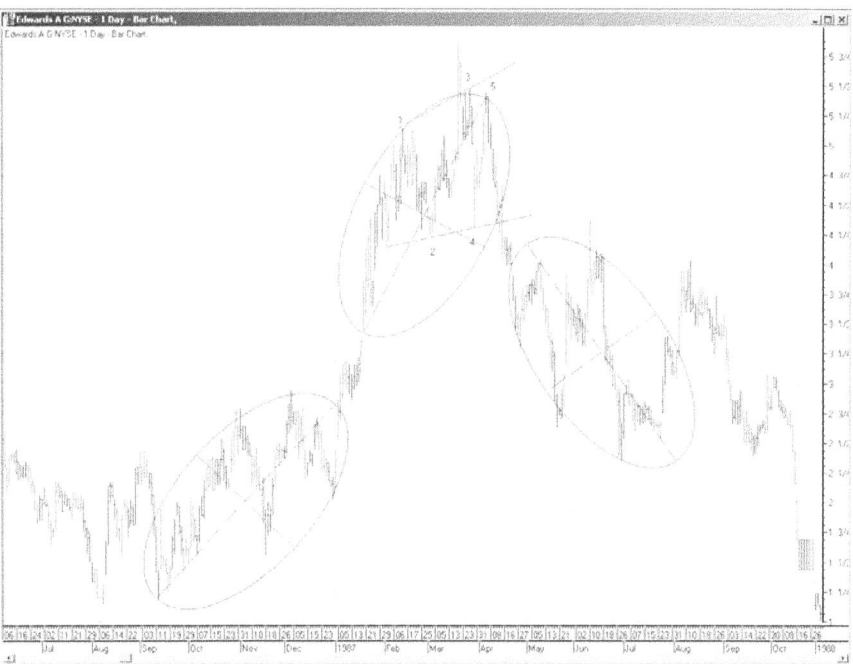

Patterns and Ellipses

THREE BUMP BOTTOM

One of the most reliable signals is a three-bump bottom. If you see the next chart the formation always starts with two thrusts down and finally one last thrust with more power. After you have that sequence of thrusts, the market turns back to the upside again. Strategy would be to buy the 3rd bottom once you have your ellipse clearly set. You could also wait for a breakout of the ellipse and buy on the first reaction in the first upward trading ellipse.

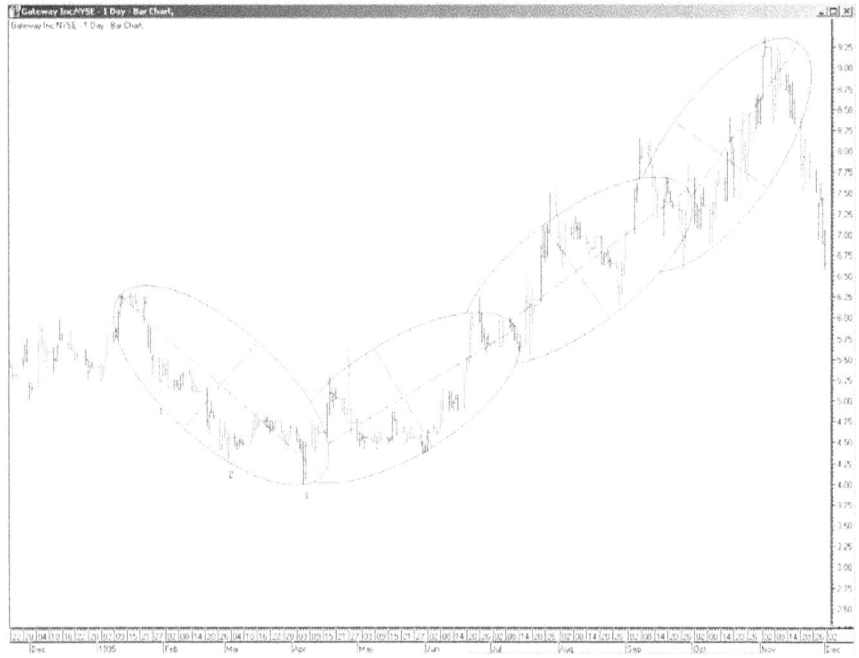

THREE BUMP TOP

Just like we had a three-bump bottom, we can also have a three-bump top. The best strategy is to try to sell the 3rd top. Try to find the next ellipse and sell into it.

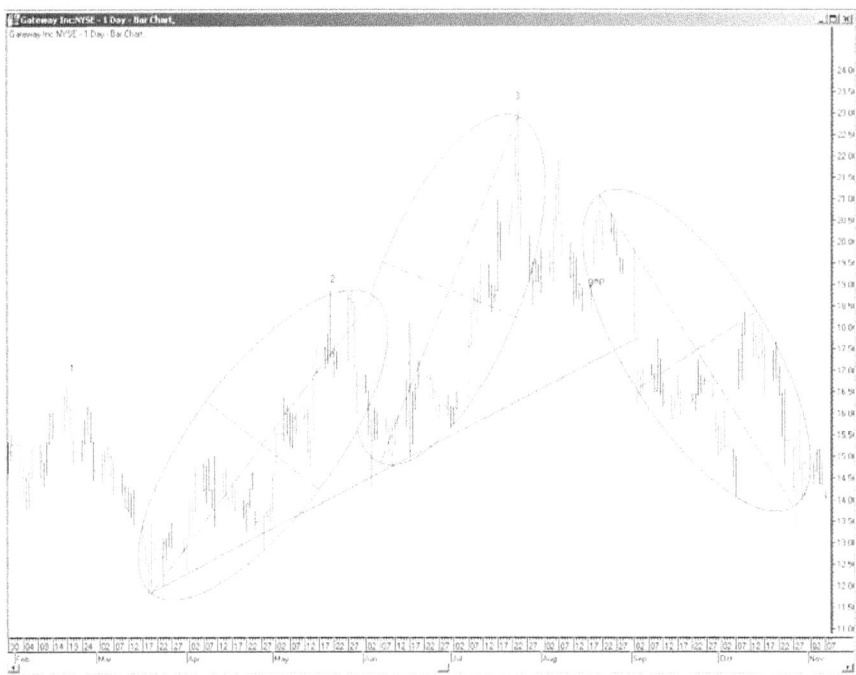

Patterns and Ellipses

CUP AND HANDLE

The cup with handle is a formation where you have a big rounded bottom and start to rise then prices break out and fall back to the cup lip. In the following example I have used ellipses to give you an idea how the cup forms in one. Also I have places a small ellipse over the cup handle. The best strategy to use is to buy when prices come back to the cup lip. Follow the prices with moving stops from there on.

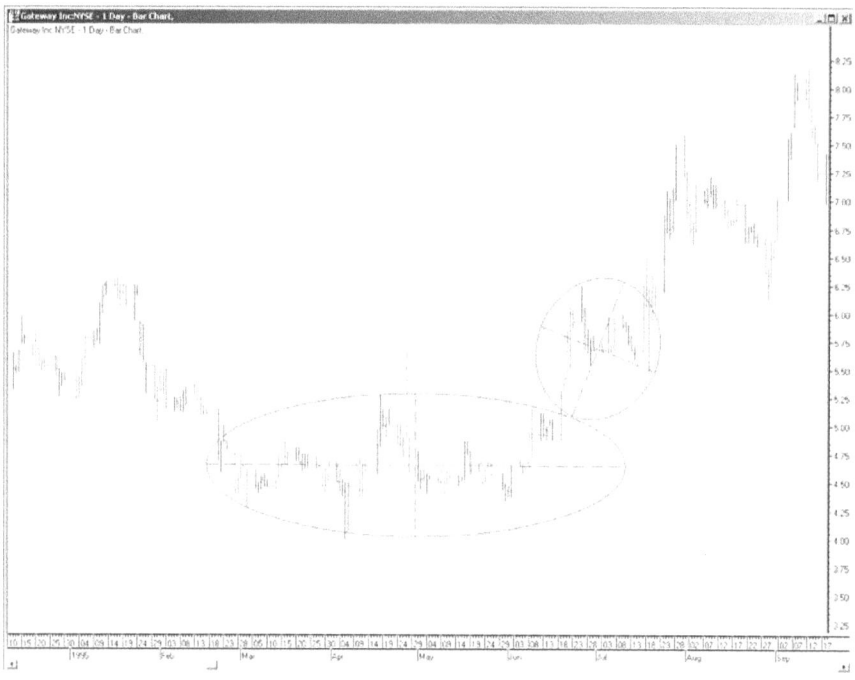

GAP & BOUNCE

One thing to look for in volatile markets is the gap and bounce. It usually occurs because of a news event. The market will gap down or up with a large space between previous day's prices. It will continue to move and have a slight reaction or recovery high in the case of a downtrend. This is where to take a position in the direction of the big gap. You can place the ellipse at the bottom of the gap in a downtrend. See chart below. In a up trend you would place the ellipse at the top of the gap. Strategy would be to take profits at the bottom of the ellipse.

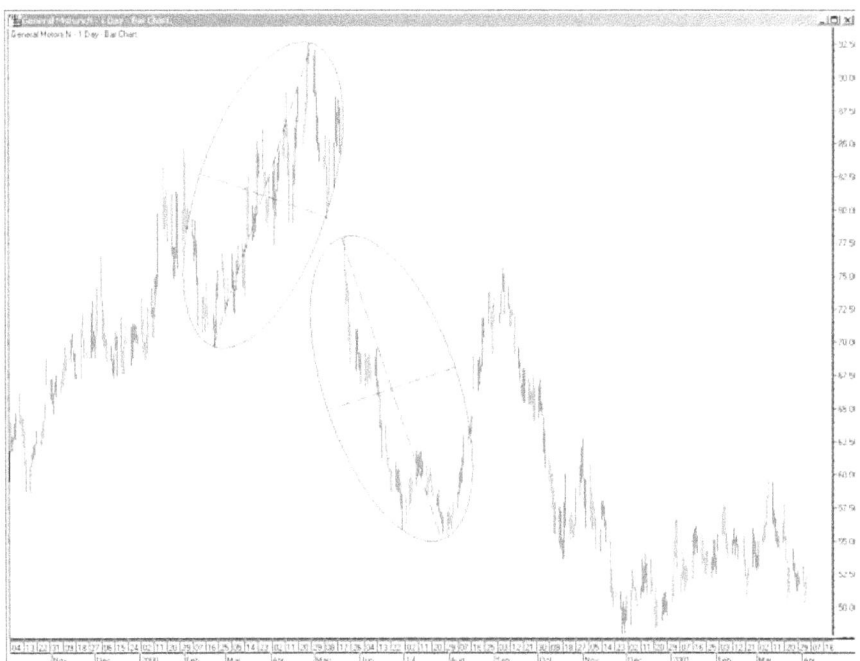

Patterns and Ellipses

DIAMOND TOPS AND BOTTOMS

The diamond tops and bottoms occur when almost a small head and shoulders formation appears and forms inside a diamond outline. In some cases sides 1, 2, 3 and 4 are equal, but not necessary. In the case below when prices break out to the downside it's objective is determined from the distance from the head to the bottom measured from the right apex. In many cases it has an expected bottom from a near term previous bottom. Strategy would be to short it when it breaks out of the diamond and take profits at it's objective, the previous expected bottom line or the bottom of the ellipse.

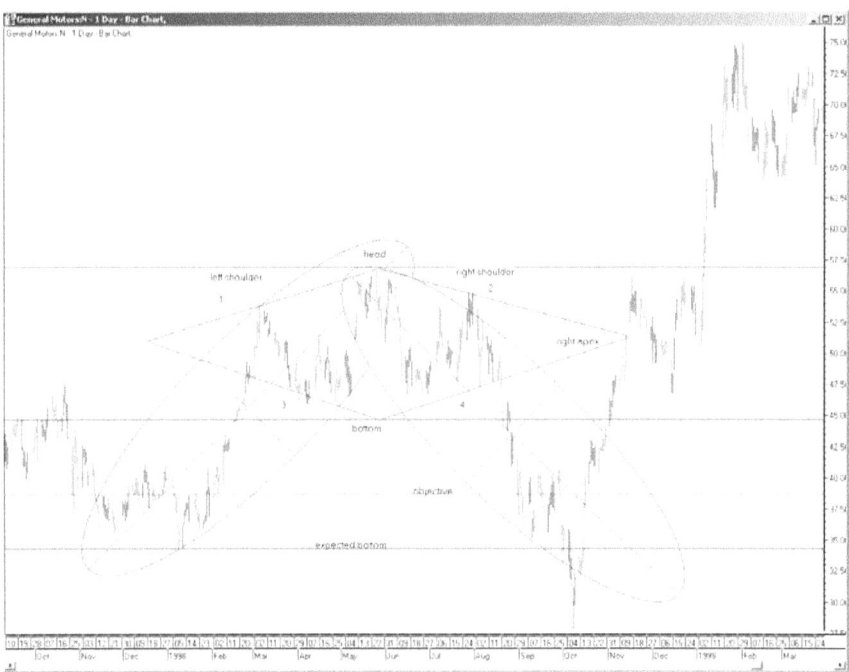

DOUBLE BOTTOMS

Double bottom occur at nearly the same level. The middle of the formation has a high and this is the confirmation line for a potential breakout. When a breakout occurs you can buy the first pull back to the breakout line. Use close stops for your protection. Your objective measurement is taken from the first bottom or second bottom to the confirmation line. Measure up again from the confirmation line the same distance. You can also use previous tops to take profits on and the ellipses the market is working with as objectives. In this case the market accelerated upward with a lot of velocity. The breakaway gap indicated much higher prices until we finally had the exhaustion gap, which signaled the end of the trend.

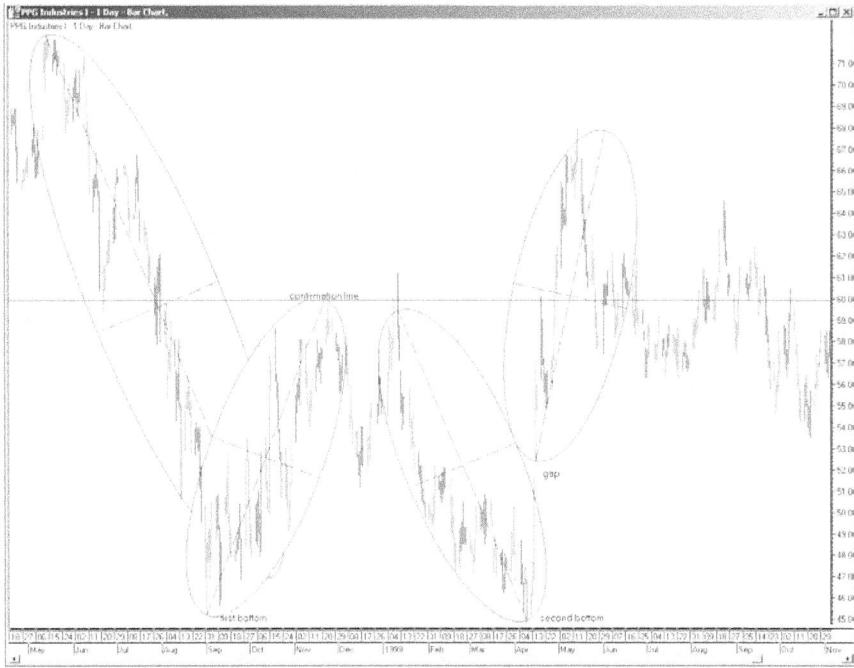

Patterns and Ellipses

DOUBLE BOTTOM FAILURE

In this case a double bottom formed and was somewhat sloppy. It finally broke over the confirmation line and went to the end of the projected ellipse and failed. The ellipse was projected from the gap that occurred after the second bottom. Since it already made it's ellipse objective when it broke out it was not a buy.

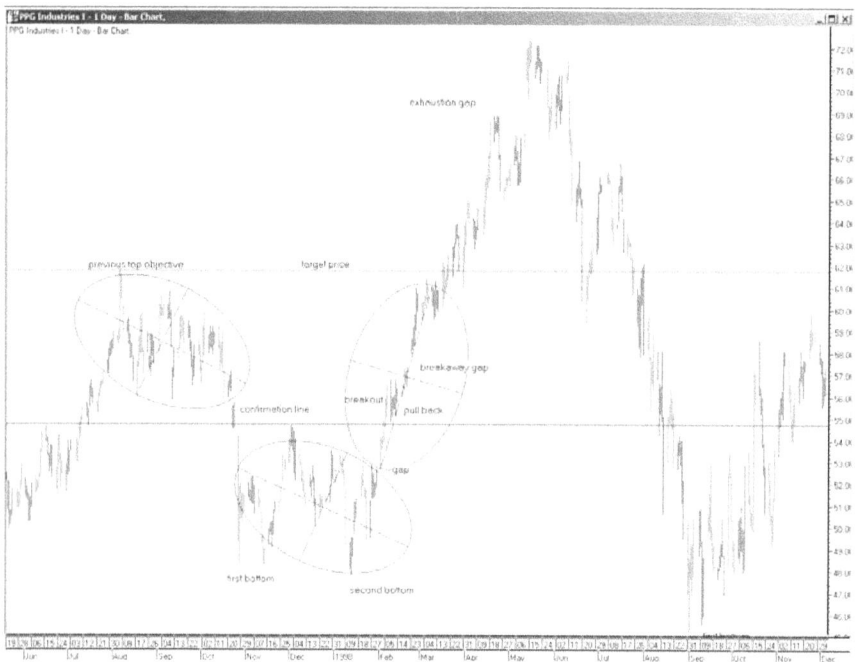

DOUBLE TOP

In this example of a double top it was very clear when it broke its confirmation line. It had an excellent pull back to short on. There was no gap, so the ellipse indicated it's objective down to the previous projected low. Prices dropped rapidly down to the ellipse's objective and ended right after the exhaustion gap occurred near the bottom.

Patterns and Ellipses

PENNANTS

These types of formations are short in duration and go the direction of the main trend. They are usually a pause in the direction. You can usually buy the breakout of the formation and sellout at the objective. The objective is measured from the start of the trend to the middle of the pennant formation. The same distance is then measured up from the same point. In this case there was also a gap allowing an ellipse to be placed in such a position as to indicate the same objective as the one from the pennant measurement. Also in this case we had a three-bump top ending at the top of the ellipse.

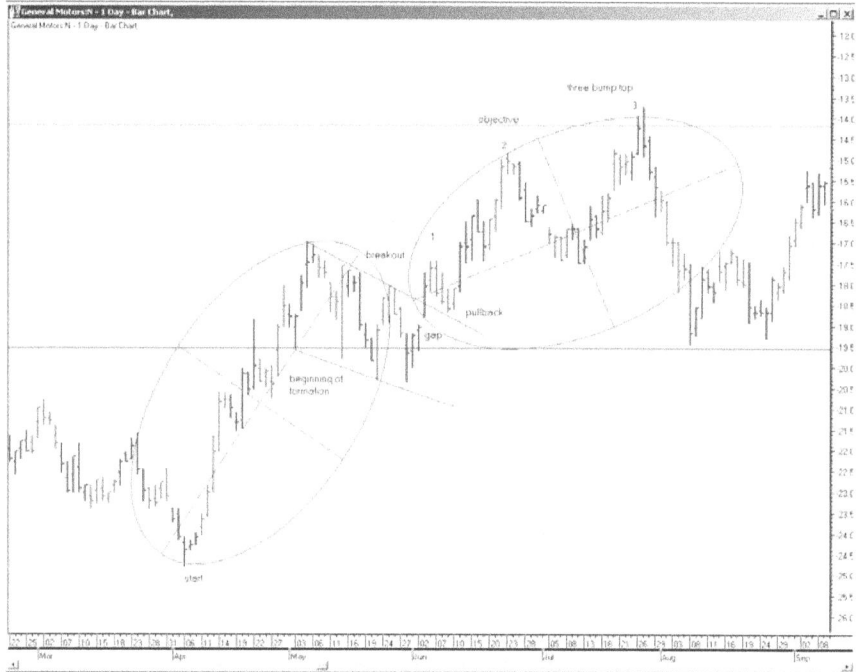

FLAGS

Flags are about the same thing as pennants. The formation comes to a point instead of being open. The measurement technique is the same. The measurement from start to the middle of the flat is taken. Then project this up the same amount to give you your objective. In this case an ellipse was created giving the same objective. The ellipse was started from the gap. See chart below. Also notice the three-bump top indicating the end of the uptrend.

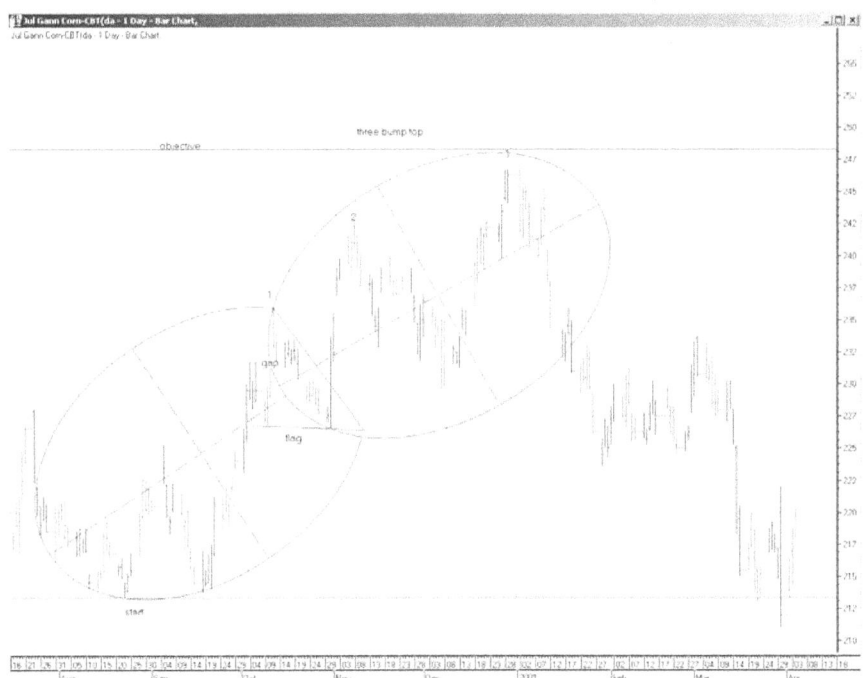

Patterns and Ellipses

HEAD AND SHOULDERS BOTTOMS

The head and shoulders bottom is formed by three thrusts to the downside. The left shoulder and right shoulder are usually higher than the head. The neckline comes off the left shoulder high and hits the right shoulder high. When a breakout occurs it usually falls back to the neckline or even below it sometime. The stop should be placed under the support of the bottom right shoulder. The objective after the breakout is the distance of the head from the neckline forecasted up the same amount. The previous high is also an objective as is the objective of the ellipse formed after the gap occurred from the buying pullback.

HEAD AND SHOULDERS TOP

Here is an example of a Head and Shoulders Top. It formed with three failing thrusts to the upside. The head was higher than the left or right shoulder. The price fell back to the neckline several times. Strategy would be to short after the break under the neckline. Keep stop close. Objective would be the head and shoulders objective, the previous near term low objective and the end of the ellipse. The ellipse was placed on the last gap.

Patterns and Ellipses

INSIDE BAR

The inside bar is a bar with a price range narrower then the day before. You must wait for the direction of the breakout and go with it. It usually produces a small move. Ellipses can be used in conjunction with this signal for short-term objectives.

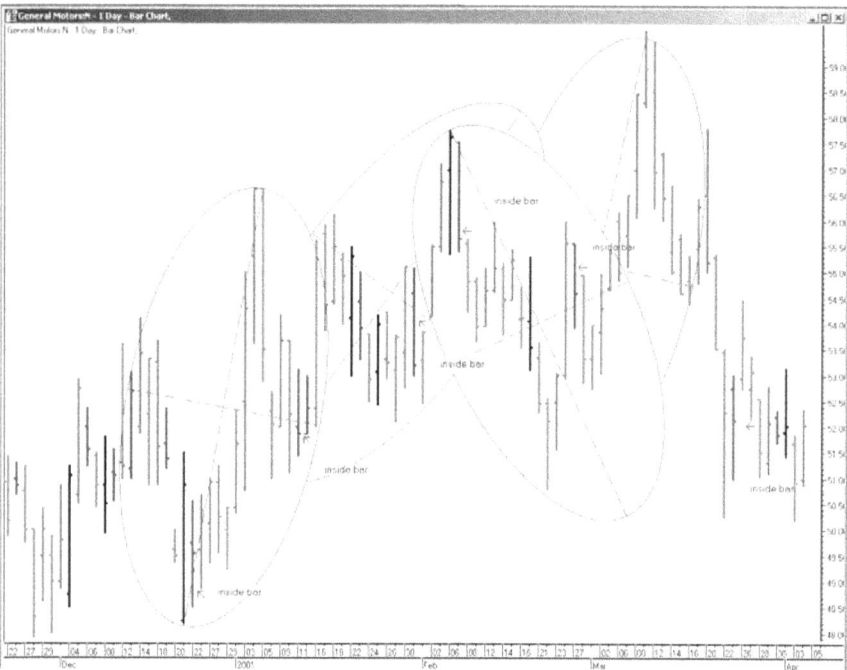

ISLAND REVERSALS

This is a formation where prices gap up into and then gap down out of. The formation is rather rare. When you do find one it is usually news driven. You should watch carefully for gaps to use ellipses on to measure objectives from.

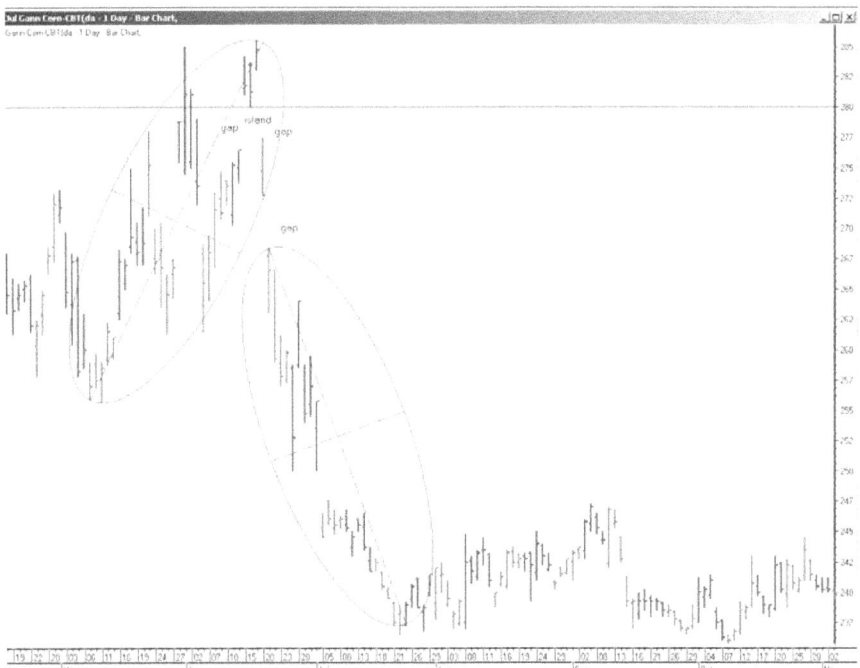

Patterns and Ellipses

MEASURED OBJECTIVE DOWN

Using measured objectives if fairly reliable. You merely take the first move down A to B and wait for the reaction to C. You then add the same distance A to B on to C on the downside. You also tie into the projection of the previous low, which is near the same measured move.

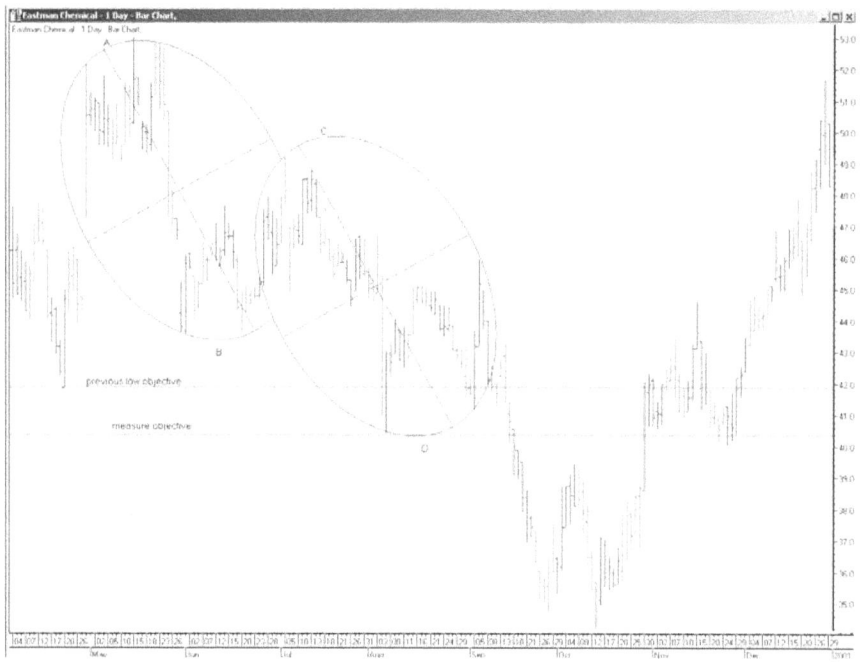

MEASURED OBJECTIVE UP

Using the same technique as the Measured Objective Down except in reverse you take the measurement of A to B and add it on to C giving you D, the Measured Move Objective. Add also the previous high objective to give you a second point.

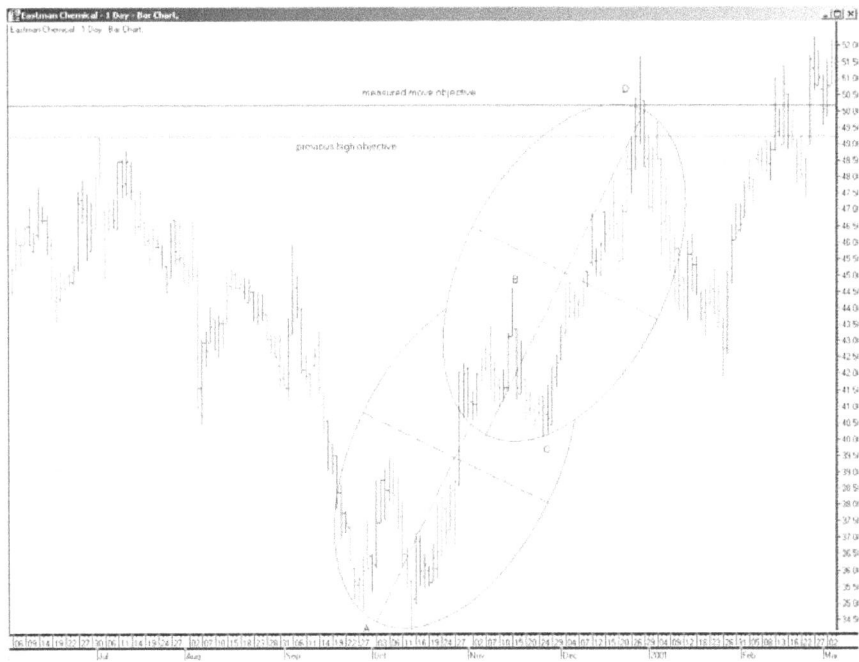

Patterns and Ellipses

ONE-DAY REVERSAL

The one-day reversal is a signal that is usually good for a few days of a price move. In this case we tided it in with an ellipse for a downside objective.

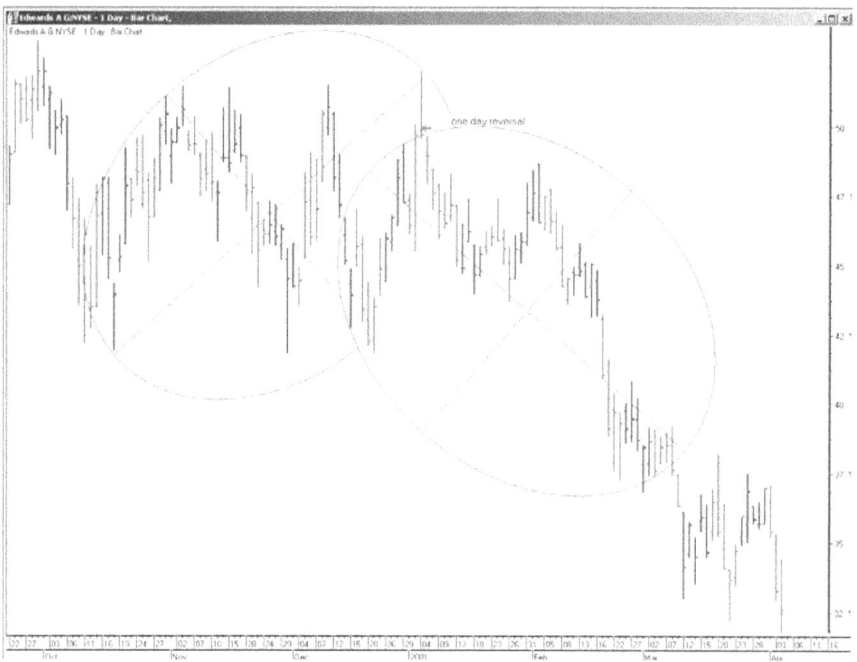

OUTSIDE BAR

The outside bar is a bar that has a higher high and lower low than the day before. Just like the inside, it will many times give a price reversal that lasts a few days. You should go with the breakout in the direction of the move. Other techniques should be used with it for price projections.

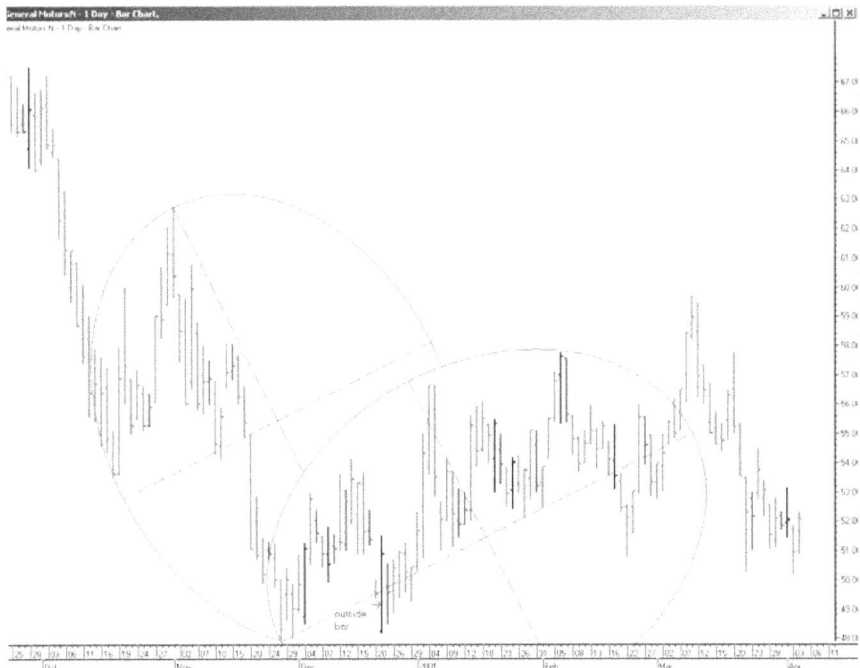

Patterns and Ellipses

TWO REVERSE BARS

These are two adjacent bars stuck up or down out of the formation. They usually give a minor move in days. Sometimes these two bars stick out of the ellipses to a small degree. In the following example three are given which gave very good price moves.

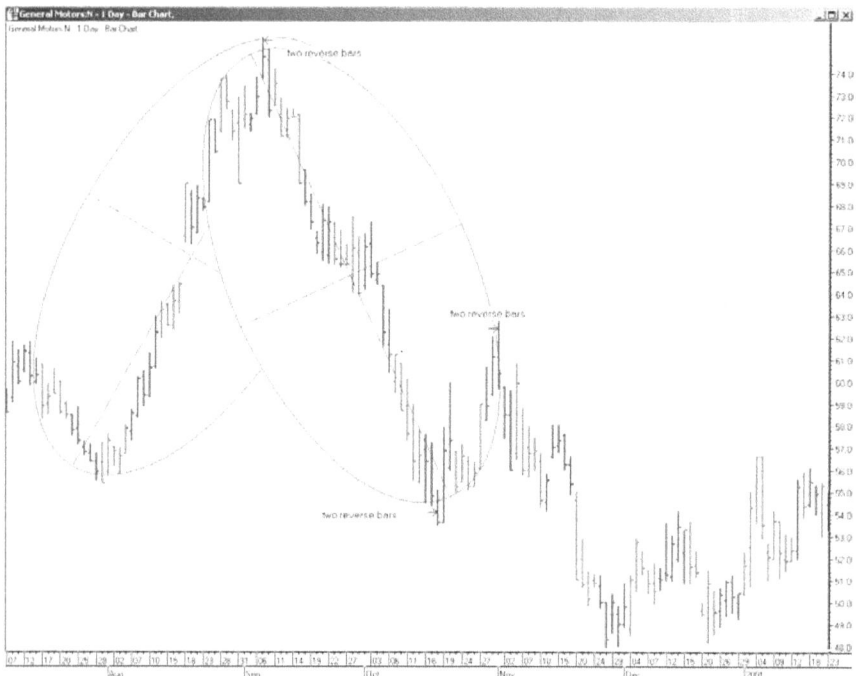

TWO REVERSE BARS ON WEEKLY CHARTS

The same two reversal bars that work on daily charts also work to a better degree on weekly charts. Ellipses can also be used as a measuring device on these charts also.

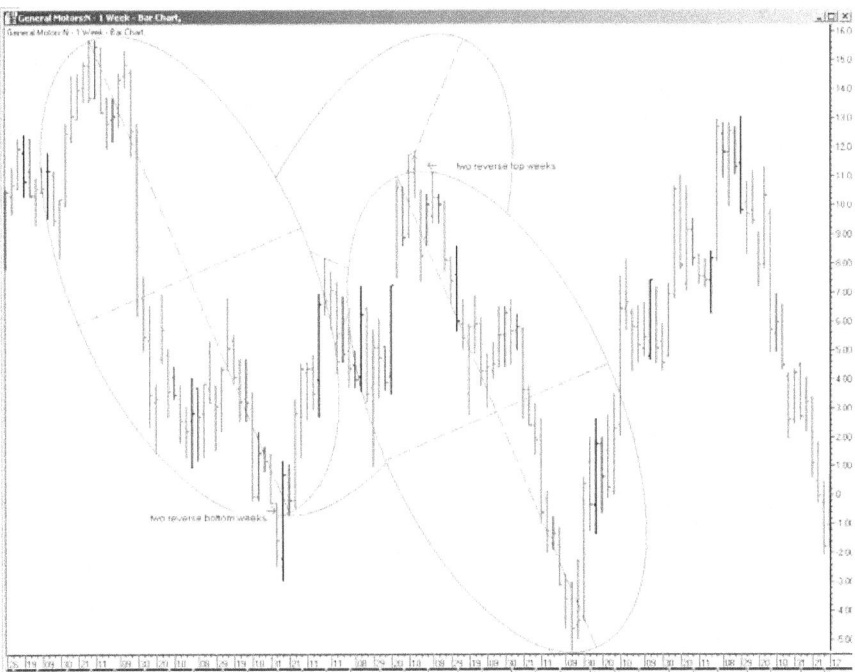

Patterns and Ellipses

RECTANGLE BOTTOMS

Rectangle bottoms are very reliable. The longer the width the more reliable they are. It's best to have at least two touches on the top and bottom of the rectangle. In this case we had six touches. When the breakout first occurs, 90 percent of the time you will have a pullback to buy. The minimum objective is the height of the triangle. The maximum objective is the width of the rectangle. You can tie in other things like a near term pervious high and the objective of the ellipse.

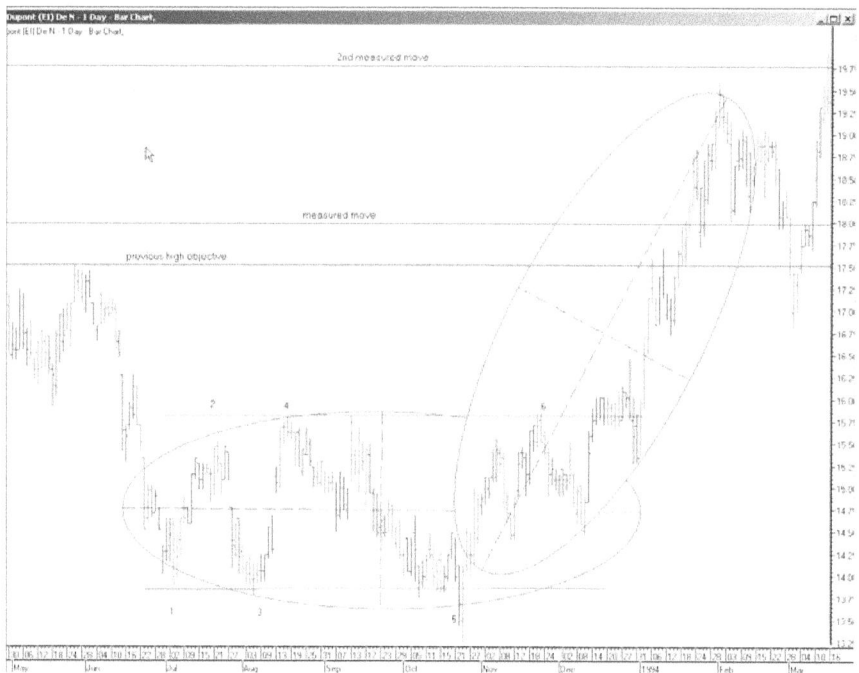

RECTANGLE TOPS

Here is an example of a rectangle top. It's just the reverse of the rectangle bottom. It needs at least 4 hits on the rectangle to make it valid. When it breaks down short on the first reaction. One objective is determined by the rectangle height, a second objective is determined by the triangle width. The previous low is another objective as well as the ellipse objective.

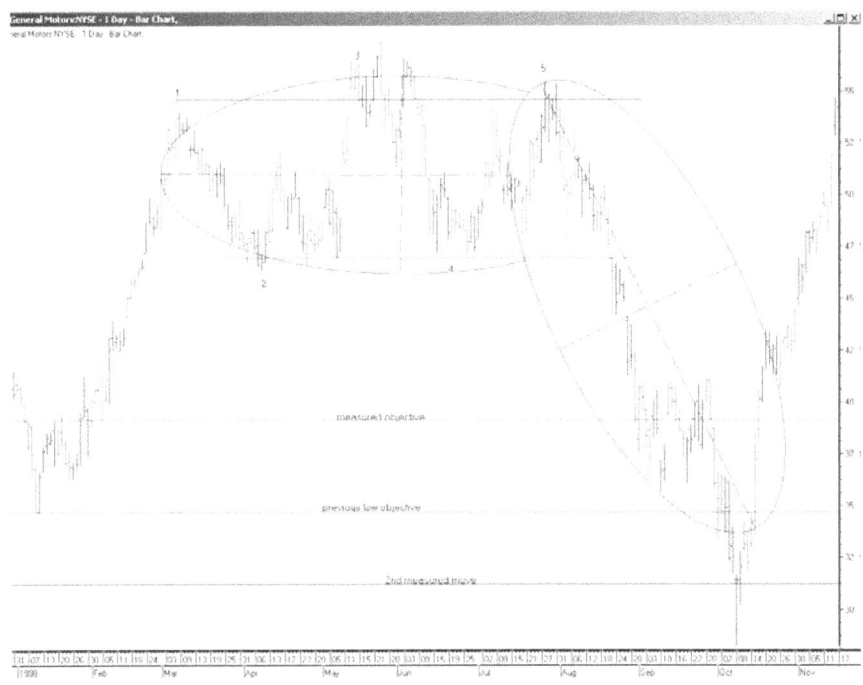

Patterns and Ellipses

ROUNDED BOTTOM

The rounded bottom is a good signal. Normally you should wait for it to break out of the top of the rounded bottom. Buy the first reaction. The measured objective is the height of the rounded bottom added to its top. The ellipse also gives you another measurement for a potential move.

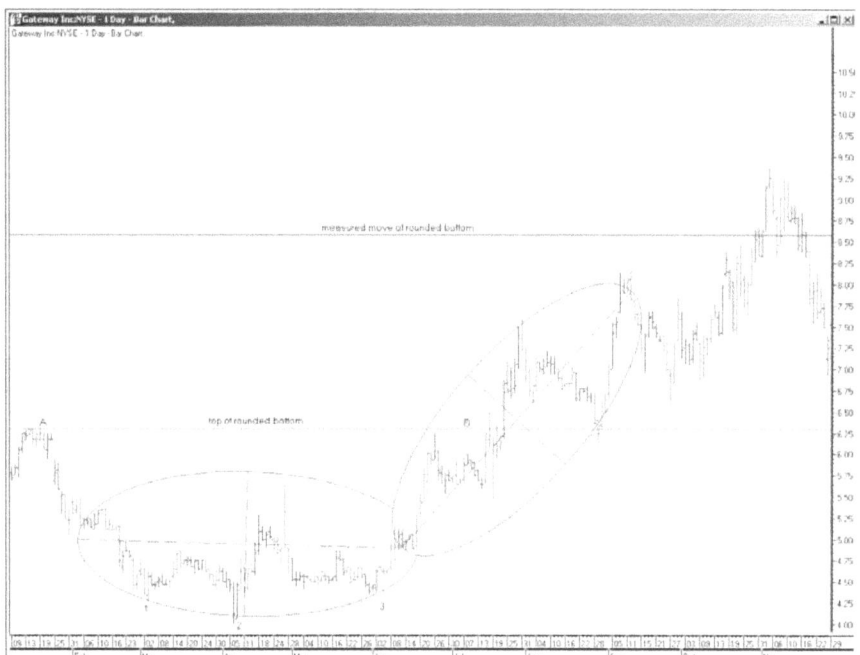

ROUNDED TOP

The rounded top is the opposite of the rounded bottom. Once the formation forms and breaks out under the bottom of the rounded top it can be shorted usually on a reaction. The measured objective is the distance from the top of the rounded top to the bottom added on to the bottom of the rounded top.

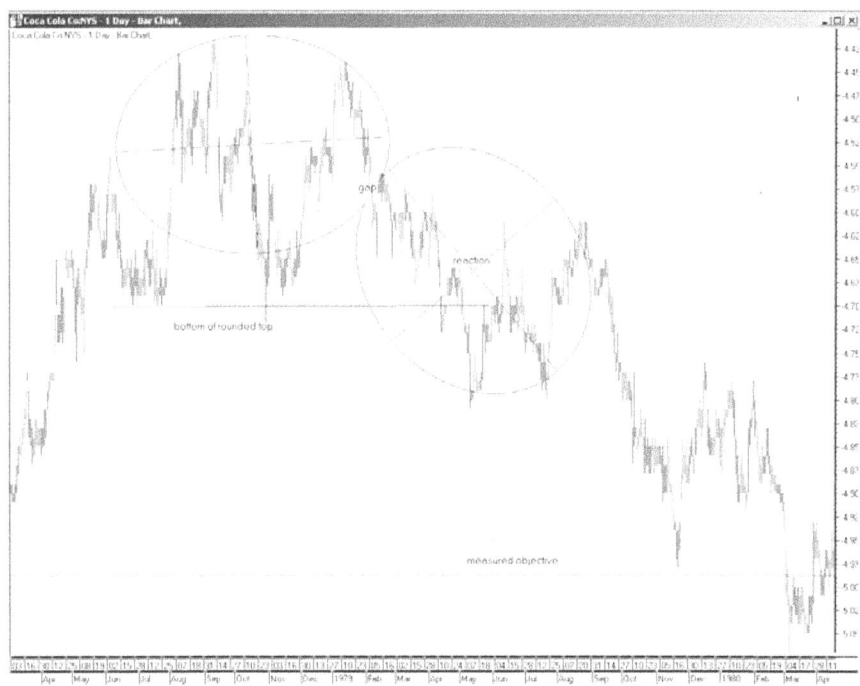

Patterns and Ellipses

ROUNDING CORRECTION UPTREND

This is a minor type of a correction in an upward move that has a rounding bottom. Try to buy at the bottom portion of the round bottom. The objective is the top of the measured move, which is taken from the bottom of the ellipse to the top add on to the bottom of the next ellipse.

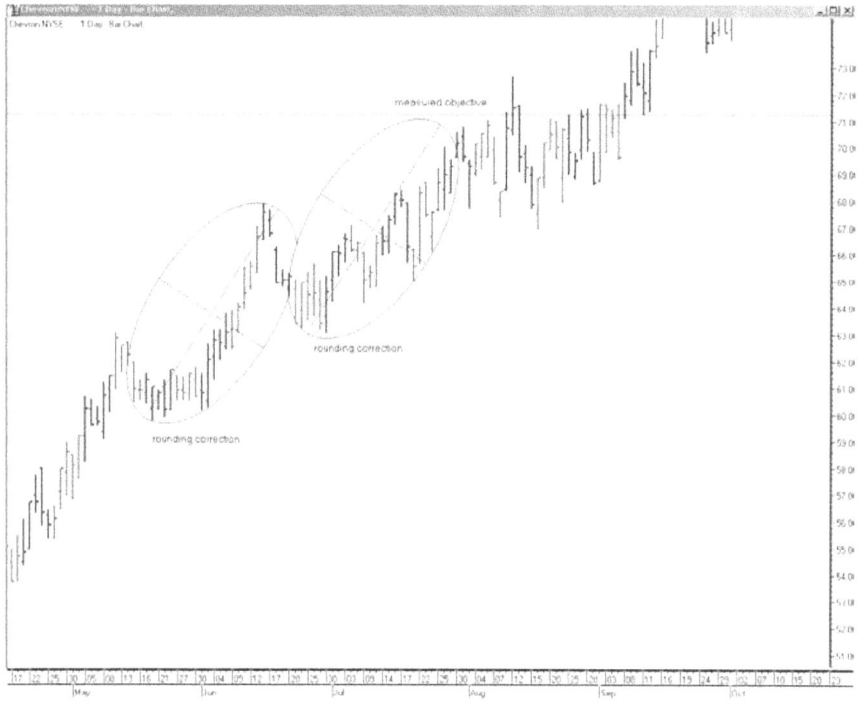

Larry Jacobs

ROUNDED CORRECTION DOWNTREND

You can also have the same rounded correction in a downtrend. The measured objective is taken from the top of the ellipse to the bottom and added to the top of the next ellipse for the projection. In this case there was a gap in which a new ellipse was created as much lower prices were indicated.

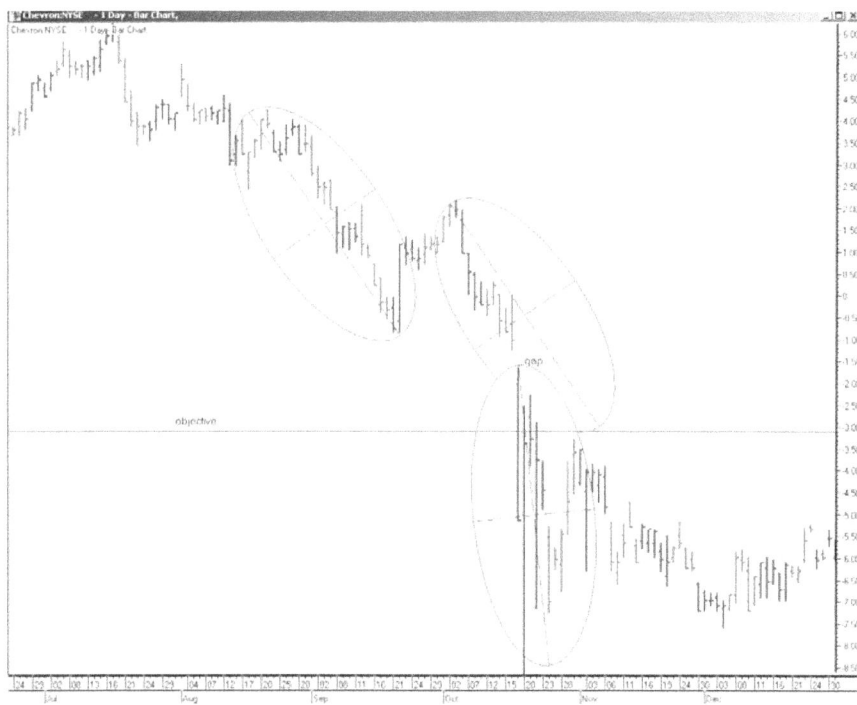

Patterns and Ellipses

ASCENDING TRIANGLE

The ascending triangle is a very common formation in an uptrend. You need at least three points to hit in the formation. The next measured move is taken from the difference of the top of the triangle and the bottom of the triangle added to the breakout point of the triangle. It can also be bought when it breaks out of the triangle and has its first reaction.

DESCENDING TRIANGLE

The descending triangle formation is the opposite of the ascending triangle formation with the same type of rules. In this case the market formed the descending triangle. It broke out on the downside. It could have been shorted on the break with the first reaction. It did not make its measured move initially, but it did make the ellipse projected move later on. Later on it also made it's descending triangle measured move.

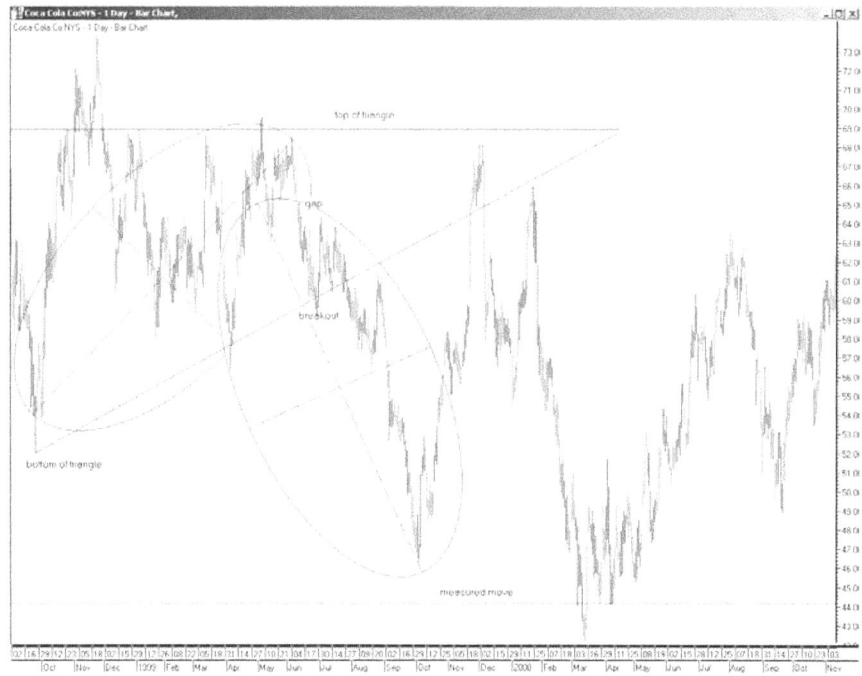

Patterns and Ellipses

SYMMETRICAL BOTTOM TRIANGLES

The symmetrical bottom is a continuation triangle in the direction of the main trend. You can buy breakouts of the triangle in the direction of the trend. Buying the first reaction can also be done. Measured objectives can be taken from the breakout point using the high to low measurement of the triangle at point A.

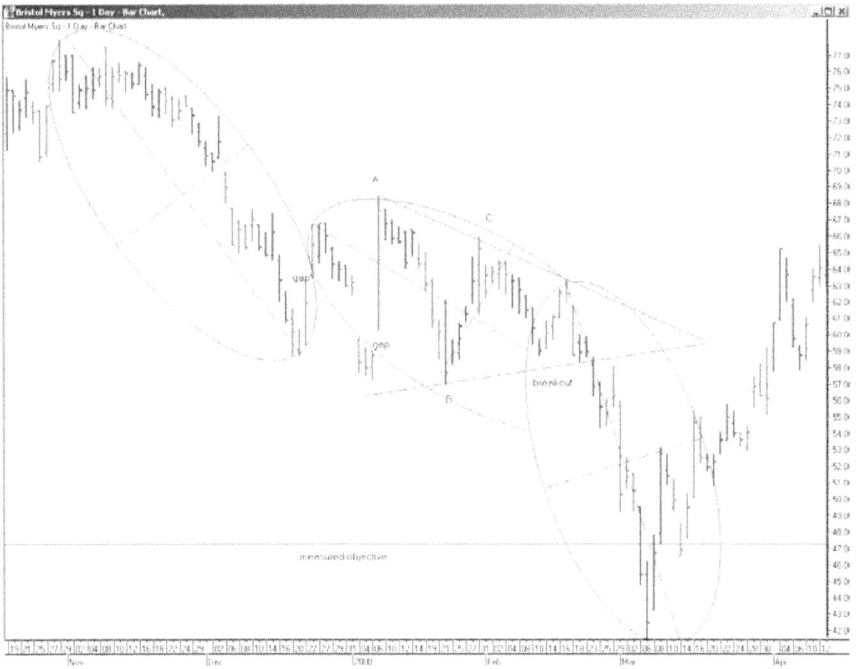

SYMMETRICAL TOP TRIANGLES

Symmetrical top triangles are small triangles in the direction of the main move. You can buy breakouts, which usually go to the measured objectives taken from the height of the triangle at the widest point from the breakout point. In this chart the first move up out of the triangle hit the measured move exactly.

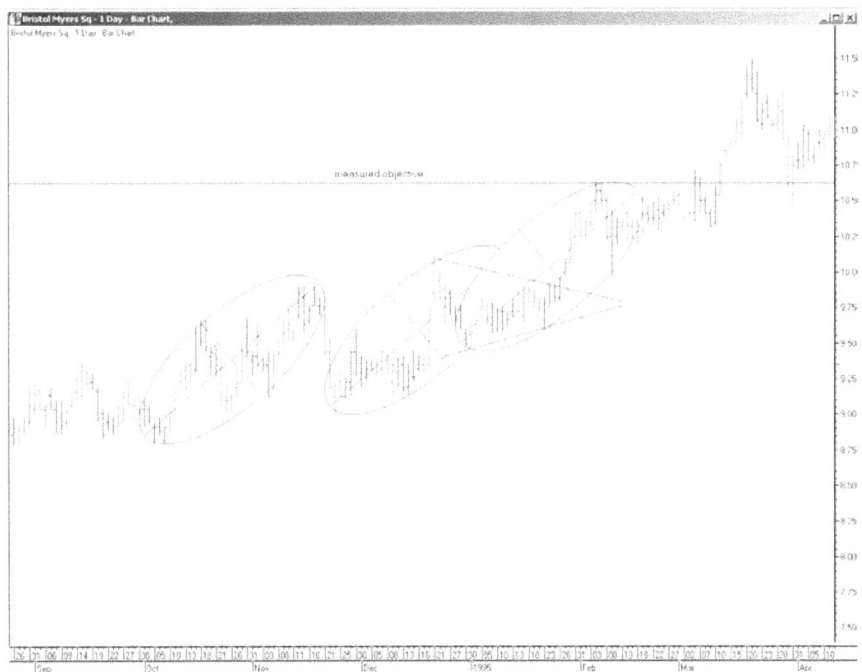

Patterns and Ellipses

TRIPLE BOTTOMS

Triple bottoms are excellent pattern formations. The buy is a breakout about the breakout line and a slight pullback. The measured objective is taken from the lowest point in the triple bottom to the breakout line and added to the breakout line. The ellipses can also be used for objectives.

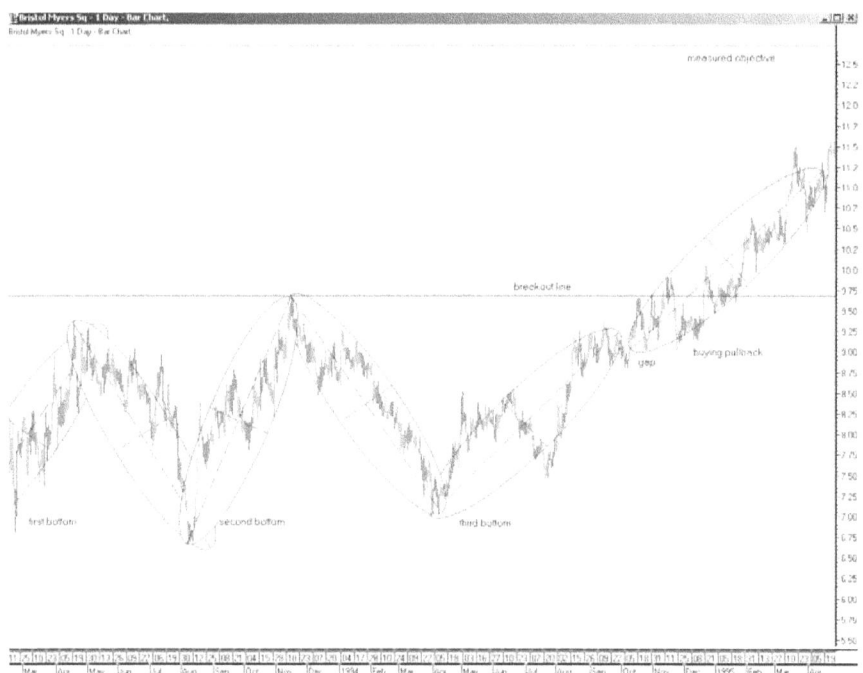

TRIPLE TOP

The triple top is another excellent formation. The signal to go short was given when prices penetrated the breakdown line in this example. Wait for the pull back to enter. To find the measured objective find the highest top down to the breakdown line and subtract it from the breakdown line. Also note how good the ellipses measured the move.

Patterns and Ellipses

FALLING WEDGE

This is an excellent wedge formation, which has two downward slopping trend lines. It can be bought on a breakout of the downward slopping trend line after a slight reaction. Measured objective is taken from adding the widest part of the triangle added on to the breakout point. In this example the previous high was also an objective, which it did hit. The ellipses also did a fine projecting job in this example.

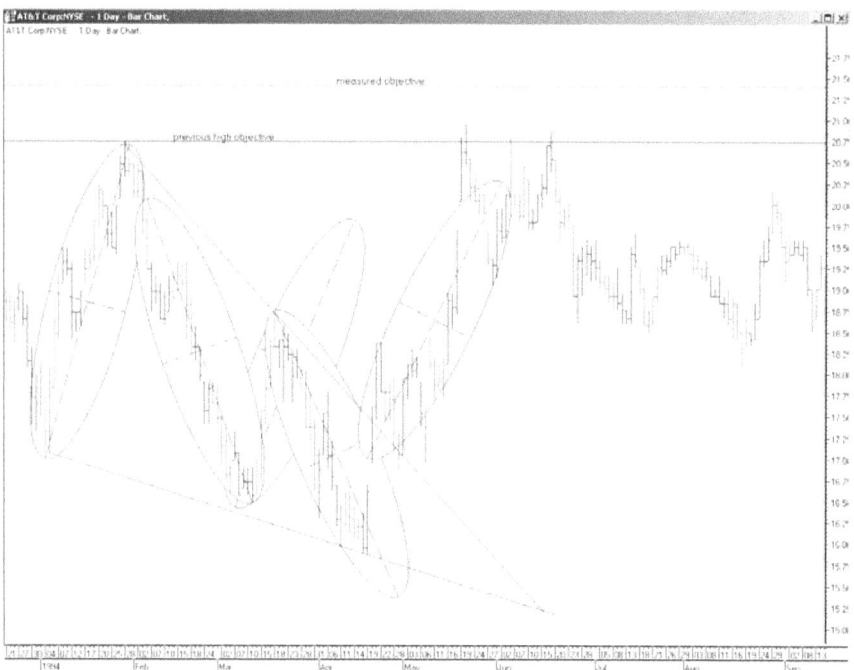

RISING WEDGE

This is a bearish pattern in a downtrend. You can short the breakout of the lower trend line. The measured objective figured from taking the widest part of the wedge and subtracting it from the breakout point on the downside. After it broke out of the wedge it gapped giving us a clear place to put the ellipse. The market finally made its measured objective later on in the chart.

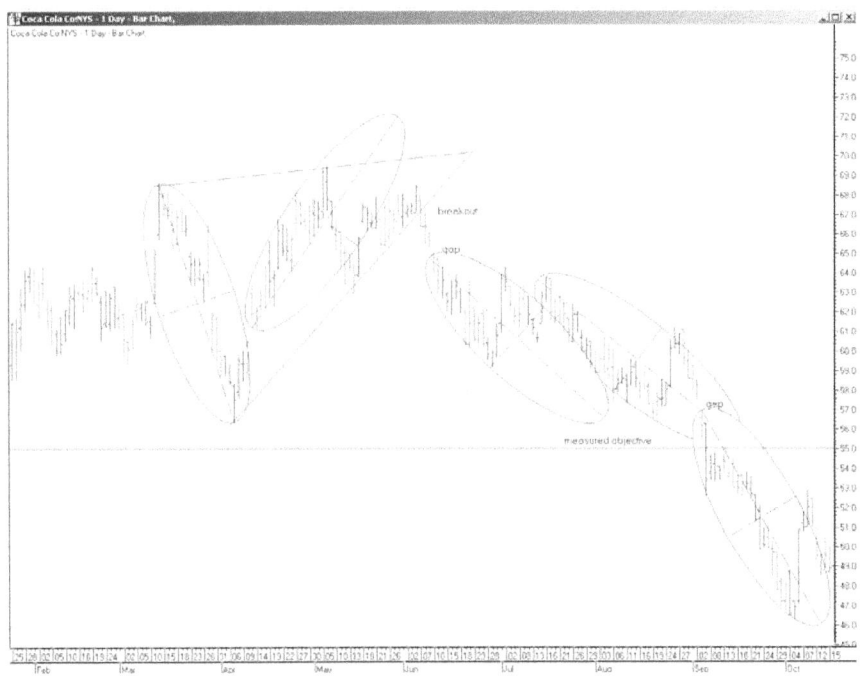

Patterns and Ellipses

REVERSAL BAR

A reversal bar is when the market makes a higher high and lower low and closes under the prior days low. The market can be shorted on the close of the same day with a stop over the high of the day.

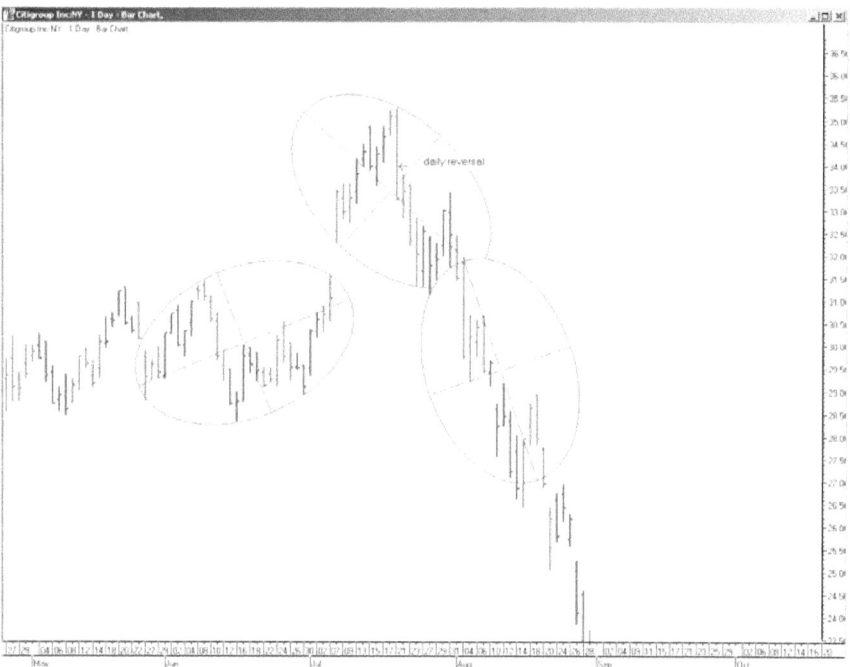

SUMMARY

This book was written to help you with Ellipses and Patterns and many of the other techniques available in the arena of technical analysis. You should study the techniques carefully to see if you might integrate them into your own trading system. The system you use should be an accumulation of all the techniques that you have found to be useful in your own method of trading. You should also back test any method you get to make sure that it has the reliability that you feel is necessary to trade successfully.

The market master Mr. George Bayer developed many of the techniques that were illustrated in this book in the late 40's. Recognition should be given to this man. He spent years studying the works of the ancient philosophers and poured over hundreds of charts to develop his trading theories.

All of the techniques illustrated in this book were taken from charts produced from the Market Analyst II software. Market Analyst III will be out by the time this book is published and will have many new significant features.

The Market Analyst is the only known software package that can create and manipulate ellipses on technical analysis charts. It can also perform multiple Gann and astrological trading techniques on charts unlike any other package on the market. You owe it to yourself after reading this book to take a 30-day free trial of the software.

Patterns and Ellipses

COPYRIGHT July 2012

No part of this publication may be reproduced, stored in a retrieval system or transmitted in any form or by any means, electronic, mechanical, photocopying, recording, scanning or otherwise.

Parts of this book came from the ELWAVE software manual produced by Prognosis Software Development. This publication is written to provide accurate information in regard to the subject matter covered. It is sold with the understanding that the publisher is not engaged in rendering professional services. If professional advice or other expert assistance is required, the services of a competent professional person should be sought.

CAVEAT: It should be noted that all stock and commodity trades, patterns, charts, systems, etc., discussed in this book are for illustrative purposes only and are not to be considered as specific advisory recommendations. Further note that no method of trading or investing is foolproof or without difficulty, and past performance is no guarantee of future performance. All ideas and material presented are entirely those of the author and do not reflect those of the publisher or bookseller.

All charts in this book were from the Market Analyst II with permission of

Market Analyst, PO Box 265, Albany Creek 4035, QUEENSLAND, AUSTRALIA

Library of Congress Cataloging-in-Publication Data:

Printed in the United States of America

Larry Jacobs

www.ingramcontent.com/pod-product-compliance
Lightning Source LLC
Chambersburg PA
CBHW071756200526
45167CB00017B/313